Out of the Doghouse for Christian Men

Complimentary copy
provided by Marnie C. Ferree
615-467-5610
www.BethesdaWorkshops.org

Out of the Doghouse for Christian Men: A Redemptive Guide for Men Caught Cheating

ROBERT WEISS LCSW, CSAT-S
MARNIE C. FERREE LMFT, CSAT

FOREWORD BY DAVE CARDER

Copyright © 2018 Robert Weiss and Marnie C. Ferree

All rights reserved.

ISBN-13: 978-1985135123 (paperback)
ISBN-10: 1985135124 (paperback)

All rights reserved. Printed in the United States of America. No part of this publication may be reproduced, stored in a retrieval system, or transmitted in any form or by any means, electronic, mechanical, photocopying, recording, or otherwise, without the written permission of the publisher.

Publisher: Three iii Publishing
             197 W Via Lola, Unit 11
             Palm Springs, CA 92262

Cover design by Sandy Flewelling
Interior design and formatting by Scott Brassart

PRACTICAL NOTE

The descriptions and examples in this book purposefully do not identify specific individuals or their stories. Since confidentiality lies at the very center of the psychotherapeutic relationship, we have taken the most exacting measures to preserve the privacy of real people. All names are fictitious, and other recognizable features have been changed. Furthermore, the people and circumstances portrayed in these pages are composite in nature. Each case represents a great many individuals whose characteristics and experiences have been adapted conceptually, carefully altered in their specifics, and combined to form illustrative viewpoints, characters, and stories. Any resemblance of such composites to actual individuals is entirely coincidental.

CONTENTS

	How This Book Came About	1
	A Note to Cheating Men	7
	A Note to Betrayed Spouses	13
	Foreword, by Dave Carder	17
1	Defining Cheating and Relationship Infidelity	19
2	Well, Okay, I Guess You Could Call It Cheating	39
3	How Women (and Men) View Relationships and Betrayal	57
4	What to Expect from Your Betrayed Partner	71
5	To Stay or Go?	87
6	Seven Ways You Can Make a Bad Situation Worse	107
7	Your Way Out of the Doghouse	121
8	Creating a Commitment Plan	141
9	Eight Ways to Make Things Better	155
10	Beyond the Doghouse	181
	Addendum: About Disclosure	193
	Further Reading	199
	References	203
	About the Authors	207

HOW THIS BOOK CAME ABOUT

I have long known and respected Rob Weiss as a colleague and now a friend. For probably two decades, his has been a powerful, intelligent, and articulate voice advocating for the clinical treatment of sexual addiction. Although we are different in many ways, and at times we come from opposite ends of the spectrum regarding certain issues or viewpoints, we have forged a respectful and warm relationship, for which I am very grateful.

Rob and I spoke together a few years ago at a conference of the International Institute of Trauma and Addiction Professionals (IITAP), and we shared with the audience some of our personal processing about the presentation. First, we stated our obvious differences:

>MCF: I'm female.
>RW: And I'm not.
>MCF: I'm straight.
>RW: And I'm not.
>MCF: I'm Christian.
>RW: And I'm definitely not.
>BOTH: chuckles (accompanied by audience giggles and smiles)

Those differences prompted Rob's invitation to revise his original version of *Out of the Doghouse*. He is smart enough, savvy enough, and most important, open enough to realize that more conservative readers would likely bypass his book because of their disagreement with some of its fundamental premises, such as the freedom to do anything one likes sexually as long as it is fully consensual and legal. At the same time, without a hint of judgement, Rob recognized that Christians, too, desperately need this type of practical guide. As one who has spent my entire life in conservative Christian circles, I couldn't agree more. I have seen countless Christian marriages and homes, including my own, devastated by infidelity. I'm honored and humbled by the opportunity to reframe this superb book within a Christian worldview.

After the audience at our presentation had quieted down and we had shared a supportive hug, which generated more laughter, Rob and I outlined the things we have in common. Professionally, we are alike in our commitment to helping people who have experienced problematic sexual or relational behavior. Combined, we have worked in this field for over 50 years. Personally, we are passionate about our commitments to a way of life that involves integrity, transparency, fidelity, empathy, connection, and spirituality. We may define some of those concepts differently as they relate to sexual behavior, but the foundational principles are fully shared. This respectful footing creates positive collaboration, which is a grace.

My adaptation of *Out of the Doghouse* maintains the powerful structure of the original book as a practical, realistic guide to the process of accepting responsibility, understanding the pain of those hurt by infidelity and offering them heartfelt empathy, and re-earning trust. This book is intentionally not meant to be a comprehensive treatise of "healthy sexuality" from a Christian worldview; that just isn't its purpose.

I'm assuming the reading audience consists of those who have clearly deviated from any Christian's definition of a standard for healthy sexuality (or have been hurt by someone who has). If you are frustrated by the absence of certain "litmus test" definitions, please keep reading. More importantly, I invite you to do the work outlined in these pages, as I believe that process is readers' most important current priority. I further invite you to wrestle with God and self about thorny issues that often generate controversy in religious communities.

Without question, sexual health springs from an intimate relationship with God and a commitment to mold one's life accordingly. Consider the advice the apostle Paul provides to the Christians in Rome:

> "[H]ere's what I want you to do, God helping you: Take your everyday, ordinary life—your sleeping, eating, going-to-work, and walking-around life—and place it before God as an offering. Embracing what God does for you is the best thing you can do for him. Don't become so well-adjusted to your culture that you fit into it without even thinking. Instead, fix your attention on God. You'll be changed from the inside out. Readily recognize what he wants from you, and quickly respond to it. Unlike the culture around you, always dragging you down to its level of immaturity, God brings the best out of you, develops well-formed maturity in you." (Rom. 12:1-2 The Message)

Most other Bible translations use the word *body*: "Offer your bodies as a living sacrifice, holy and pleasing to God—this is your true and proper worship" (New International Version). Often, commentators extrapolate that language to target what we do with our bodies sexually. I certainly don't disagree that if our bodies are, indeed, the "temple of the Holy Spirit" (1 Cor. 6:19), it is wise to be prudent about what we do with them sexually and with whom we do it. I love, though, Eugene Peterson's expanded description in The Message that goes beyond bodily or sexual things. It fits perfectly with Rob's premise in *Out of the Doghouse*: Infidelity is much more than simply doing this or that with your body! Likewise, rebuilding trust with those harmed is much more than just not doing certain things sexually. Even a quick read of the following pages makes these points clear. I have teased Rob that he wrote a much more "Christian" book than he realized. Truth is truth.

At the same time, I recognize that some parameters for defining healthy sexuality are probably expected, and I hope are unanimously shared by all Christians. From our faith or "holiness" perspective, these basics are central to our beliefs, and thus, to our understanding of what follows in *Out of the Doghouse*:

- Our sexuality is the highest incarnation of our spirituality. I believe that in sexual connection, we can feel most linked to the divine.
- Full expressions of sexual connection are sacred and reserved for the sanctity of a covenant marriage. Sex, then, is intended as a celebration of the union of two loving people who are committed to monogamy.
- Sex is the highest, deepest, and most lasting communion, and potentially the most pleasurable and playful connection possible. God designed sex to be AWESOME!
- Sex is the joining of minds and spirits as much as bodies. It is not to be degraded by objectification or a reduction into a focus on body parts or specific activities. Pornography, then, is detrimental to healthy sexuality and viewing it (or engaging in other forms of casual or anonymous sex) is a violation of the partners' covenant relationship.
- Sexual activity is always based on safety, trust, honesty, and respect. It is not meant to be degrading or intentionally painful.
- Men and women are equal partners within a sexual relationship. Women aren't expected to "give" while men are freely entitled to "take." The connection and pleasure of both partners is the common goal. Again, healthy sex within a covenant relationship is AMAZING!

4

Accompanying the desire that this Christian version of *Out of the Doghouse* avoids controversy about potentially divisive issues surrounding appropriate expressions of sexuality, I have an equally strong intention for this adaptation: This book will not provide judgement for those who have fallen short of Christian values regarding sex. You'll find no name-calling or put-downs here. Nor will you find the wagging of long, bony spiritual fingers at sexual sinners. Yes, violating the sacred sexual trust of a marriage is a sin in theological terms. But throwing shame-flames into a burning fire doesn't help extinguish it. Men deservedly in the doghouse because of their sexual betrayal are eligible for the lavish grace of a loving God, as thankfully are we all.

Out of the Doghouse for Christian Men seeks to provide what the subtitle promises: a redemptive guide for Christian men who cheat. This is a practical book much more than a religious one. Yet Christian principles and scripture undergird pragmatic steps toward healing, which is an eternal truth never more clear than in an area as important as sexual integrity. I pray men who have cheated will find a helpful path of restoration, and I pray their wives will find validation for their pain, along with a roadmap of realistic expectations about when their husbands might be ready to leave the doghouse. The rest of the redemptive process is up to God.

—Marnie C. Ferree
Founder and Director, Bethesda Workshops

A NOTE TO CHEATING MEN

Before you charge ahead into the meat and potatoes of this book, we want to tell you what you're getting into. Basically, this is a book written for heterosexual Christian men who have cheated on a woman they love, have gotten caught, and don't want to lose their relationship with her. This content might be useful for anyone else who has harmed a loved one by cheating, but the focus of *this work* is husbands (or straight men in a significant relationship like an engagement) who have strayed and want to make things right. Period.

Nevertheless, we fully expect that women, rather than men, will be the primary purchasers of this book. Specifically, we're talking about the hurt, angry, and traumatized wife or girlfriend who just learned that her man is sleeping with a neighbor or a coworker and possibly several other women that she doesn't know about yet. Put another way, after more than 25 years as therapists specializing in sex and intimacy issues, particularly serial infidelity, our naiveté is gone, and we no longer expect the cheater to be the one who reaches out for help. How could we, when experience tells us that 99 percent of the time it's the betrayed spouse who insists on change?

So, if you're reading this book, it's highly likely that you're doing so because your wife or fiancée gave it to you (or perhaps threw it at you) with a suggestion like, "Read this, you hateful jerk, or I'm leaving!"

We do know that some men will buy this book of their own accord. If you did that, good for you; there is a very good chance that the information offered herein both can and will help you save your relationship. But, as we've said, the odds are high that you didn't make the purchase, and instead you got this little guidebook from your seething spouse. Either way, you're almost certainly clueless about two very important things: (1) the types and degree of pain that your cheating has caused her, and (2) the concrete steps you must take to save your relationship. These are the primary topics this volume addresses.

Of course, what you choose to do with this information is up to you. It's possible that you will read this through and think, *Nope! I'm not doing any of that.* If so, your relationship may not survive. And even if you take the direction and advice provided within these pages and follow it to the letter, there is no guarantee that things will work out. This fact is sad but true. The pain wrought by your cheating might be too much for your loving partner to forgive, no matter how much you love her.

A crucial spiritual principle applies here: *surrender*. To achieve ultimate healing, your deepest work is to surrender the outcome of this process to God. In recovery language, which has been our wheelhouse for decades, you are powerless over whether your wife will take you back or not. You can't make her do *this* or not do *that*. What you can do is allow a loving God to be in charge of the outcome, and focus on doing what you can do, which is to carefully and thoroughly follow this guide. Most likely, especially if your wife has gone to the trouble of providing you with this recipe for saving your relationship, not only can you repair it, you can make it better than ever. And that is a redemptive possibility! Be encouraged and read on.

> Note: Throughout this book we will use certain terms interchangeably. For instance, *wife*, *spouse*, *partner*, *mate*, and *loved one* will all be used in reference to your primary

life partner, the woman you've betrayed. When referring to your relationship with this woman, we will use *marriage, relationship, intimate connection,* and various other terms interchangeably. Similarly, terms like *lover, hookup, mistress, other woman,* and *affair partner* will refer to the woman (or women) with whom you've cheated. We use these multiple terms to include engaged couples as well as married ones, and so as not to limit the kind of betrayal you may have committed to a certain description. (We also use them to avoid the boring stylistic repetition of words, which drives us both crazy.) Our goal in using various terms is to be inclusive, trusting that you, the reader, can find yourself and your relationship within these terms, whichever words we're using at any given time.

It's important that you understand that we pull no punches in this book. Why should we? You're neck deep in misery of your own making, and pretending that you're not won't do you or your relationship any good. The truth is this: If you love your spouse and you truly want to save (and even grow) your relationship with her, then you must accept and deal with the painful reality of what you've done.

Be at peace. This book isn't meant to shame you, although you may at times feel ashamed while reading it. Remember, healthy shame (also known as guilt) reminds you that there is a God, and it's not you. It's normal and even positive to feel guilty about betraying your wife in such a powerful way. That's part of facing the reality of what you've done. Toxic shame is a different thing: It cripples you with the lie that you are beyond God's love and forgiveness—that you are a horrible, terrible person. That kind of internal critical voice isn't from God and isn't helpful. In fact, it can keep you paralyzed, or worse, prompt you to return to cheating because you think you've messed up so badly that your behavior doesn't matter anymore, anyway.

- This isn't a book that judges you or treats you as if you are a bad person. The truth is that all of us do bad, terribly hurtful things; otherwise, we would never have needed a Savior to bring us back into relationship with God. This is a book about the wrongs you have done and what you can do to correct them. Read passages like Romans 8 when you find yourself in a bottomless pit of gripping shame.
- This book isn't meant to provoke you, although you may at times feel anger (and many other emotions) while reading it. When this occurs, please understand that it's a necessary and positive part of the redemptive process.
- This isn't a book that will help you justify your infidelity by exploring possible issues in your marriage, even though you may currently believe your circumstances make it understandable that you strayed. That may be helpful work for your relationship eventually, but it isn't the first step. Your job right now is to put your best paw forward to get out of the doghouse.
- This book invites you into genuine brokenness over your cheating, which is the beginning of repentance and restitution. It asks you to look at *your behavior* and the ways in which it prompted your relationship troubles, and it pushes you toward an understanding of and empathy for your spouse's emotional turmoil.

The truth is that portions of this book may be hard to read and even harder to process and integrate into your life. Furthermore, you may never be quite the same for having read it, which actually is our sincere prayer for you. This transformation is true regardless of whether your current relationship survives, because the information contained herein provides a different pathway for you. It will first show you the difference between making decisions impulsively, like the choice to cheat, and stopping to fully consider how your actions might affect others. Children act impulsively because they don't know any better; mature adults should not, because they do know better. Once you fully face the difference, there's no going back.

This is a book about living with truth and integrity as your guide, and about cleaning up the mess on your side of the street without blaming your spouse for that mess or her reactions to it. More important, this book offers you the potential not only to reconnect with your mate, both emotionally and (eventually) sexually, but also to develop your relationship in ways you never thought possible. If that is what you want from your life and your marriage, then you're reading the right book. The only question is whether you're willing to humble yourself and do the deep work of restoration.

> "Rend your heart and not your garments. Return to the Lord your God, for he is gracious and compassionate, slow to anger and abounding in love, and he relents from sending calamity." (Joel 2:13)

A NOTE TO BETRAYED SPOUSES

Although this book isn't written for you, in many ways it is about you. In fact, our primary goal here is to help your man understand the pain that his cheating has caused you, the ways in which he has violated you, and what he must do to regain your trust. Ideally, after reading this volume, he will grow in many important ways, becoming not only a better husband but a better man.

The suggestions for relationship improvement provided here are based on a combined fifty years of experience as therapists specializing in sex and infidelity issues. Over the years, we have worked with hundreds of cheating men and their betrayed partners. Based on that depth of experience, we have a very good idea of what you're thinking and feeling. We know where your pain is. We also know what your cheating spouse needs to do to make things right. So even if you don't agree with every word contained in these pages, we hope that you will trust the process of healing.

Within this work there is a rhythm, pace, and pathway to your husband's emotional redemption and your relationship healing. We ask you to put aside your understandable fears and suspicions and your potential desire to control the process. We will eventually steer your mate toward empathy and long-term behavioral change—which is possible provided he truly wants to make things right with you. Unfortunately, if he's merely going through the motions, no book (or therapist) can really help. Nor can any amount of hand-wringing, demands, or tearful challenges from you. However, if your spouse is ready to move past his cheating and develop a deeper intimate connection with you, this book can and will facilitate that process.

We suggest that you let your mate work at his pace and with his own sense of commitment, even if waiting for him is difficult. If he wants to make your relationship whole again, and if he's ready to value the life he shares with you and the commitment he made before God, the information and suggestions in this book will eventually be as effective as tipping the first domino in a well-lined-up row. All will fall, one right after another. But it takes time and effort (and sometimes outside assistance) to properly line up the dominoes. In fact, you will probably need a couple's therapist to guide you and your mate through this process. But that's secondary to what your man can learn and accomplish by reading this book and following its directions.

If you're uncertain about staying in your relationship, that's an understandable place to be. We only suggest that you be honest with yourself and your partner. Don't use your questioning of the relationship as a threat; simply let him know that your uncertainty is a reality. Of course, if you're prepared to stay with him and to make your relationship work, please let him know that, too, as it will be helpful to all concerned.

At this point you may be wondering, *Will I ever forgive him?* In our opinion, the topic of forgiveness requires a separate volume to address adequately. For now, here are some valuable starting points:

- Forgiveness is a process, not an event—often a process that's revisited as healing and time move forward.
- Forgiveness doesn't mean you weren't hurt or that what your husband did wasn't wrong.
- Forgiveness doesn't negate holding healthy boundaries and enforcing consequences.

- Forgiveness doesn't necessarily mean a restoration of the relationship. You can forgive him and still not trust him.
- Forgiveness is a gift you give yourself. It means you stand up for yourself, value your worth, and take responsibility for your own healing regardless of what your husband does.
- Forgiveness starts with an intention of your will, not with a feeling. You feel your feelings, grieve your losses, and choose to take back your power.
- Forgiveness frees you to focus on healing and embrace freedom.

Forgiveness is ultimately for you. It's not something you do for your husband. It's the key that allows you to open your heart to the joy of the moment, instead of staying stuck in the pain of the past.

One important final note: There is nothing you've done to make your man cheat, so please don't blame yourself for his infidelity (or allow anyone else to blame you). If he was unhappy or feeling lonely and unfulfilled, he had many options other than what he chose to do. Be assured that his choice to cheat is on him, not you. Nothing you have done translates into an automatic free pass on infidelity. Thus, it's important that you give yourself a break, tend to your own needs with compassion and self-care, and understand that your spouse's behavior isn't your fault and it never was.

As devastating as this period may be, please know that it can be the doorway into the kind of marriage you always wanted and deserve. Paradoxically, we find that couples who have endured infidelity and chosen to take the hard journey to repair their relationship report a deeper level of intimacy than they experienced before. As Ernest Hemingway penned, some become "strong at the broken places." As God promises, "Behold, I am doing a new thing; now it springs forth, do you not perceive it? I will make a way in the wilderness and rivers in the desert" (Isa. 43:19 ESV).

FOREWORD, BY DAVE CARDER

The field of treating sexual betrayal in a committed relationship is only about 30 years old. Prior to that, if infidelity occurred in your marriage, your only choices were to sweep it under the rug and move on in the relationship, or divorce. For 40 years I've looked for and desperately needed some reinforcement for the guys I was working with. I found it! Reading the very first chapter of *Out of the Doghouse for Christian Men: A Redemptive Guide for Men Caught Cheating*, I said, "Whoa, this is it!" This book will become a staple in my arsenal to address the tide of a culture gone sex crazy.

As we all wait for evidence-based treatment to accumulate, it's important to draw upon the experience of practicing therapists who have specialized in finding ways to help couples heal from sexual betrayal. Such are Robert Weiss and Marnie Ferree. I've been aware of Rob's work through his frequent contributions to *The Therapist* (the bi-monthly publication of the California Association of Marriage & Family Therapy). I have referred many clients to Marnie's seminal work, *No Stones: Women Redeemed from Sexual Addiction* and to the wonderful treatment program she directs, Bethesda Workshops.

But the development of resources has focused on the betrayed spouse, and very little has been provided for the betrayer. Finally, we have a book for guys, written in guy's language, from a guy's point of view, and answering the questions guys have about their recovery, their spouse, and their future.

This is a book of truth on fire, a bottom line, straight shooting, go and do healing manual. All in very clear language. If you're a cheating guy, you'll swear that you were followed, recorded, and that your never vocalized thoughts were captured in this material.

And the best thing? Christians can buy into this book wholeheartedly. You don't have to filter anything. Marnie has done a magnificent job of adapting Rob's terrific original book to integrate Scripture and Biblical concepts necessary for healing and forgiveness. It goes deep to get you by the heart, unpack the pain you've caused your wife, and challenge you to take the necessary steps.

There is no judgement in this book, no condemnation, and no effort to make you pay for what you did. You can't. But there is a lot of good old fashioned hard work that you must do if you want to come out still married and enjoying the relationship you've always wanted. You'll need directions for this journey; you can't figure this out as you go. You'll lose if you try. You just get one chance for redemption after infidelity. You don't want to live in the doghouse with an angry spouse for the rest of your years. This book provides a clear guide for the way out.

You're also afraid this process will never end, that it'll cause more ugly scars or long-lasting wounds. You wonder if you'll get through it. You will. In *Out of the Doghouse for Christian Men*, Marnie and Rob help you rebuild your wife's respect and trust in you. You'll understand her great need to know that *"You finally get what you did to me!"* When your wife believes you really see the depth of the pain your cheating caused, she'll be convinced from the inside out that you will never again sexually betray her.

—Dave Carder
Pastor of Counseling Ministries, Evangelical Free Church,
Fullerton, CA
Author of *Torn Asunder: Recovering from an Extramarital Affair* and
*Anatomy of an Affair: How Affairs, Attractions, and Addictions Develop,
and How to Guard Your Marriage Against Them*

CHAPTER 1

DEFINING CHEATING AND RELATIONSHIP INFIDELITY

> "The woman Folly is loud; she is undisciplined and without knowledge. She sits at the door of her house on a seat at the highest point of the city, calling out to those who pass by, 'Let all who are simple come in here!' she says to those who lack judgment. 'Stolen water is sweet; food eaten in secret is delicious! But little do they know that the dead are there, that her guests are in the depths of the grave.'"
> —Prov. 9:13-18

Welcome to the Doghouse

Rob has a giant bulldog named Dozer. His name is Dozer because he sleeps (dozes) a lot, and, like a bulldozer, he's enormous, a bit uncoordinated, and relatively unaware of the havoc he can wreak as a big dog in a small house. Yet he's reasonably smart—smart enough to know that certain behavior, like peeing or pooping on the floor, is a serious no-no. Nevertheless, Rob sometimes finds a puddle (or worse) on the kitchen floor. Whenever that happens he points out what Dozer has done, and then Dozer is (temporarily) banished to his dusty outdoor doghouse. The doghouse isn't Dozer's favorite place to be—separated from his human posse, his toys, and his treats, not to mention his squishy, overpriced doggy bed. But actions do have consequences, don't they?

For Dozer, these temporary trips to the doghouse are a clear message that he has misbehaved and that he needs to act differently in the future. And he does understand, in his small-brain doggy way, that if he behaves for a little while out in the doghouse, Rob will let him back inside the people house. Then, if he doesn't pee or poop on the floor, snarl at guests, knock down visiting toddlers, or eat the furniture, he'll get to stay, hanging out and enjoying life in the place that makes him feel loved, included, and very, very happy.

If you're reading these words, it's likely because *you are in the doghouse* just as Dozer sometimes is. And quite honestly, if you've cheated on your mate, you're there because you deserve it. Metaphorically speaking, you peed on the kitchen floor. Your infidelity dirtied and soiled your home, and your wife is very unhappy about it. So now you're banished to the doghouse. But hey, at least she didn't ship you back to the pound or give you to another family. At least not yet.

The difference for you and your trip to the doghouse is that you're human, which means you have more responsibility for your mistakes than a pet does. Dozer is a dog, so Rob cuts him a bit of slack and his punishments don't last very long. But you're a grown man, and what you did (understandably) feels horrible to your mate. As a result, she isn't likely to let you out of the doghouse until you demonstrate that you fully understand what you did and how you hurt her. Then you must re-earn her trust to the point where she believes that you're not going to do it again.

So, get comfy out there in the doghouse, because looking at your loved one with sad puppy-dog eyes that say, *I'm sorry, I really didn't mean it*, just isn't going to cut it. That lame apology works for your pets, and maybe for your kids if they're very young, but not for you.

What Is Infidelity?

Before going any further, we want to be very clear about what we mean when we talk about infidelity (i.e., cheating). Without our having full agreement up front about this basic definition, you are likely to be resistant to the steps outlined in this book and confused about why they're necessary.

Depending on what you've done, your definition of infidelity may not match up with ours. Yet we can assure you that our definition is very much in line with that of your significant other—and that of God. Regardless of whether you agree with this version of the truth, you absolutely must understand and come to terms with the fact that this is how your spouse sees things. (As an aside, this is Rob's original definition, not one included only in this Christian adaptation of *Out of the Doghouse*. Truth is truth.)

Infidelity (cheating) is the breaking of trust that occurs when you keep intimate, meaningful secrets from your primary romantic partner.

Think about it this way: *God is always after your heart.* Do you remember Jesus' repeated rebukes of the Pharisees and others who performed religious practices but ignored the underlying principles? In example after example, Jesus challenged people who did things for show, like effusively providing charity for the poor or praying in public (Matt. 6:1-8) without the accompaniment of an authentic spirit. He chastised the religious leaders who provided an easy tithe but neglected justice, mercy, and faithfulness (Matt. 23:23). The Lord labeled "hypocrites" those who ignored desperate needs for healing like the lame man at the pool of Bethesda (John 5:1-15) and the woman who had been sick for a long time (Luke 13:10-17) simply because that healing was needed on the Sabbath. Jesus consistently criticized following the letter of the law in such things like ceremonial washing and eating, while ignoring relationships and hospitality

(Mark 7:1-8). God goes for the jugular of the heart, not the mere mechanics of the body.

Therefore, let us repeat and emphasize this statement:

Infidelity (cheating) is the breaking of trust that occurs when you keep intimate, meaningful secrets from your primary romantic partner.

Please notice that this definition of cheating doesn't speak specifically about affairs, pornography, strip clubs, hookup apps, or any other specific sexual or romantic act. Instead, it focuses on what matters most to your partner: *the loss of relationship trust.* For her, it's not any specific sexual or romantic act that has caused the most pain. Instead, it's the outright lying, the keeping of secrets, the lies of omission, the manipulation, and the fact that she feels she can no longer trust a single thing you say or do (or anything that you've said and done in the past).

This reality fits with another crucial Christian principle: Jesus was also after the heart when it came to repentance. He was harsh in his words about people who pridefully looked down on other "sinners" and found themselves better in comparison. Consider the story of the Pharisee and the tax collector:

> "To some who were confident of their own righteousness and looked down on everybody else, Jesus told this parable: Two men went up to the temple to pray, one a Pharisee and the other a tax collector. The Pharisee stood up and prayed about himself: 'God, I think you that I am not like other men—robbers, evildoers, adulterers—or even like this tax collector. I fast twice a week and give a tenth of all I get.' But the tax collector stood at a distance. He would not even look up to heaven, but beat his breast and said, 'God, have mercy on me, a sinner.' I tell you that this man, rather than the other, went home justified before God. For everyone

who exalts himself will be humbled, and he who humbles himself will be exalted." (Luke 18:9-14).

If you're serious about getting out of the doghouse—spiritually as well as relationally—sincere humility is required. You can't be cavalier about something as serious as infidelity. You can't be defensive and protest that you only did *this* and you didn't do *that* sexually. You also can't keep a ledger of your good deeds outside the bedroom to balance the scale of your cheating. At this moment it doesn't matter how wonderful you've been with the family finances, vacation planning, childcare, birthday remembrances, random gifts, or just plain being a charming guy. When you lie and keep secrets from your spouse about something really important (like extracurricular sex) and she finds out, all the good stuff you've done immediately flies out the window. In her mind, everything else pales in comparison to your violation of relationship trust. You have broken her trust as a man and as a mate. Into the doghouse you go!

Now we'll give you some good news. Once you accept and agree that the above definition does define cheating, you are on the road to understanding your loved one's anger, threats, hurt feelings, and need for control. When she finds out that you've cheated, lied, and kept important secrets, she is going to be very angry and very hurt for a very long time.

"How long will she be angry?" you ask. Without doubt it will be longer than you would like. For now, let's leave it at that; the topic will be addressed in more detail later.

"Why is she so furious?" you ask. Think of it this way: You are the one person she thought would never knowingly or deliberately hurt her or let her down. Yet you did exactly that, and in a big way.

Welcome to the doghouse.

If you can wrap your mind around the definition of cheating, then you can also start to understand what your mate views as the most precious element of your relationship: *trust*. And that's exactly what you have broken. To reiterate, it's not any specific sexual or romantic act that has done the most damage to your betrayed partner and your relationship; rather, it's your deception, emotional distancing, secrets, and the resulting *loss of relationship trust*. For your spouse, the emotional pain and loss associated with broken trust is significantly worse and longer lasting than any physical straying you've done. You're like what Jesus described as the "whitewashed tombs, which look beautiful on the outside but on the inside are full of dead men's bones and everything unclean. In the same way, on the outside you appear to people as righteous, but on the inside you are full of hypocrisy and wickedness" (Matt. 23:27). You are deservedly in the doghouse because of your betrayal of broken trust. And you will only find your way out of the doghouse when trust is restored.

Liar, Liar

For many cheating men, the immediate and best solution to a loss of relationship trust is to continue lying about their behavior, but this time more effectively. For men whose partners either cannot or will not allow themselves to see these men as untrustworthy, this tactic can work quite well—for a while, anyway. And the men who choose this path, as they get away with their increasing lies and secrets, tend to think, *Great, problem solved.*

We'll tell you, however, something you surely already know as a Christian man: Your relationship problems are most definitely not solved by "getting away with it." Even if your spouse chooses to believe your ever-increasing lies, typically because she doesn't want to experience the pain of not believing them, she will still feel your emotional distance and unavailability, which is not good for your relationship. Furthermore, you will probably cheat again and get caught again, and your marriage will deteriorate even further. If you're not yet willing to man up with humility, continuing to lie may be the way to go. If you opt for that route, please feel free to stop reading and to politely hand this book back to your mate, or to throw it in the trash, or to give it to some other poor guy in the doghouse—preferably a man who is motivated to make changes. Understand, of course, that you're also throwing away your commitment to be the man God has called you to be.

If, however, you desire long-term healing and maybe even a chance to make your relationship better than ever, we suggest you continue reading. But do so knowing that this book is about much more than getting out of a tight squeeze with some fast talking or some shallow promises. It's about the development of honesty, masculine integrity, genuine intimacy, and meaningful connection. It's about developing an open and vulnerable (yes, vulnerability is a good thing) connection with your wife. And it's about being able to look at yourself in the mirror and feel good about the man who's looking back. To reap these rewards, you'll have to man up, accept the consequences, and change your behavior in lasting ways.

First and foremost, of course, you must offer a "broken and contrite heart" to God and to your spouse (Ps. 52:17). To do so, you likely need some more definitions and information about infidelity.

Types of Cheating

Perhaps it hasn't crossed your mind yet, but there are countless ways to cheat. Typically, though, infidelity falls into one or more of the following three categories:

1. Sexploration (purely sexual)
2. Booty calls (emotionally connected but casual)
3. Full-blown romance (deeply emotionally connected, long-term affairs)

These possibilities are explored and explained below. It's very likely that you'll recognize your own behavior and thinking patterns somewhere in this discussion.

Sexploration (Purely Sexual)

Joey has been married for eight years and is in church every Sunday. Nevertheless, he has profiles on several hookup apps, and he engages in sexting frequently with women he meets through them. He likes how affirmed it makes him feel to have multiple women wanting to connect with him, including sexually. He's had casual sex several times with women he meets through these apps, which he feels guilty about and takes great pains to hide from his wife. However, Joey rarely exchanges personal information of any kind. In fact, he doesn't even share his real name with his hookups. He tells himself that he loves his wife and what he's doing isn't hurtful to her because the other women mean nothing to him. He thinks of them as "an aid to masturbation," like online pornography. He also believes his extracurricular activity keeps him from bugging his wife for sex all the time.

When asked what extramarital sex looks like, many guys think of sexploration: purely sexual activities that lack any sort of emotional component or connection, like Joey's activities in the example above. Sex for sport, you might call it. These guys often think that because it doesn't mean anything to them on an emotional level, it's not cheating, and their spouses really shouldn't care about it. When they slough off the guilty feelings, they view chasing tail as roughly the equivalent of driving an off-road vehicle, climbing a mountain, working out, or winning big at fantasy football. It's just something that guys do for fun and distraction.

We can assure you, however, that your significant other views the situation quite differently.

Sex Is…

Many men believe that complete vaginal penetration is required before an activity qualifies as sex and, in turn, as infidelity. They say things like, "If there's no vaginal penetration, it's not sex, and if it's not sex, it's not cheating." Regardless of your thoughts on the matter, we can guarantee you that your loving partner doesn't think this way. As far as she is concerned, hand jobs, oral sex (both giving and receiving), heavy petting, making out, kissing, and even just flirting can and do qualify as sexual activity and cheating. Ask yourself the following: *If my wife could watch my behavior with other women, are there parts that she would object to?* If the answer to this question is yes, then what you are doing almost certainly qualifies as infidelity, even if you'd like to think it doesn't.

If cheating is a purely sexual endeavor for you, you are right at home in our sexually saturated culture. The simple truth is that lots of men who cheat operate in this fashion. Whether you're perusing porn, hiring prostitutes, sexting with strangers, bopping the local barista, or using hookup apps for random sex, it's entirely possible that you feel no emotional connection to the women you've cheated with. To you, they are sexual adventures—no more, no less. And it's possible that you've defended yourself to your wife with a statement along the lines of, "I swear I wasn't cheating, honey, because it never affected my love for you."

If you've tried this or a similar line, we would be willing to bet that your spouse's response wasn't what you hoped for. This is because women typically view sexual attraction, sexual desire, sexual activity, and intimate connections differently than men do. Women are driven as much by emotional connection as by physical sexual arousal, and they have a difficult time separating and compartmentalizing the two. Most men are quite the opposite.

Whether there's an ancient survival-of-the-fittest component still at play or merely a cultural bias, men are more easily able to separate sex and relationship. Cavemen, perhaps, found it normal and even necessary to spread their seed around freely. In biblical times it was the norm for men to have multiple wives and concubines, though the Bible also describes relationship difficulties, such as Abram's wife Sarai and his concubine Hagar (Genesis chapter 16).

Whatever the reason, when it comes to sexual desire and sexual activity, men and women consistently view the world differently, even if those differences are unconscious. As a result, your non-emotional, purely sexual actions are difficult for your mate to fathom, and your protestations that "it meant nothing" don't and won't register with her.

When you're in a committed and supposedly monogamous relationship, being sexual with other women violates the trust your spouse has placed in you. You made a promise, through marriage vows or some other vow, either explicit or implied, that you would be monogamous with your significant other. You didn't have to make this promise, but you did, and this promise included a vow before God if you are wed. Your mate took you at your word, you reneged, and she is rightfully angry about that betrayal. Now you're in the doghouse.

To sum up: The problem is not just that you had meaningless sex with other women. The problem is that you lied, kept secrets, and broke an important commitment to your primary life partner. And because of that behavior, she no longer trusts you.

Booty Calls (Emotionally Connected but Casual)

Robert has a high-powered job that requires a lot of travel to major cities around the world: New York, London, Paris, Tokyo, and elsewhere. When he travels, he occasionally meets women that he finds attractive. When the attraction is mutual, he goes to bed with them, reasoning that what his wife doesn't know can't possibly hurt her. If the sex is good, he looks the woman up again whenever he's in that city to see if she's available and wants to get together. Several of these women are now "regulars." However, between trips he doesn't think about or contact these other women because he loves his wife and children very much.

You may, like Robert, have a string of casual sex partners that you see repeatedly but only when convenient. You enjoy the company of these women, and you may even have occasional formalized dates with them, like going to dinner or a movie before jumping into bed. But there isn't a deep emotional connection. At most, these relationships are a series of recurring booty calls. There may be some friendship and there is lots of hot sex—think of the "friends with benefits" arrangement from your college days if you're old enough to remember that description—but there is very little in the way of meaningful emotional intimacy. Most likely, both of you are aware that the sex isn't exclusive, and neither of you thinks it's "going somewhere."

If this is the way you've been operating, you may have tried to defend yourself to your spouse with lines like, "It wasn't a real affair. It was never anything more than sex. She means nothing to me." And your mate most likely got even angrier because, as discussed above, she just doesn't think or operate in that fashion.

Full-Blown Romance (Deeply Emotionally Connected Affairs)

Bret is a junior executive at a large accounting firm. Two years ago, he was assigned to work on an important account with an attractive female colleague. They quickly found out that they worked well together. In fact, their pairing was so successful that they were jointly assigned several other accounts, which put them in close contact almost constantly during work hours. Their professional relationship became, in time, a friendship, and then a close friendship in which they confided intimate details about their lives—even occasionally complaining about the various problems in their (mostly good) marriages. Eventually, at one particularly intense work-related conference, their friendship turned sexual. Bret now feels stuck, because he cares deeply about both women. He doesn't want to leave his wife and kids, but he doesn't want to end the affair, either.

With an emotional as well as a sexual affair such as Bret's, cheating might be something you never intended to do. You were simply going about your business, being nice to the people around you, making friends as you went, and not worrying too much about whether those friendships were with men or women because you were already happily married. Unfortunately, platonic relationships—in the workplace, online, in the neighborhood, or anywhere else—can unexpectedly blossom into something more. Without good boundaries, self-discipline, and effective accountability, the line between innocent friendship and cheating gets crossed.

Some therapists specializing in infidelity and couples work suggest using the concept of "walls versus windows" as an analogy when helping unfaithful partners understand both what happened to them and what their betrayed spouses are thinking and feeling. Author Shirley Glass explains this concept as follows: "You can have intimacy in your relationship only when you are honest and open about the significant things in your life. When you withhold information and keep secrets, you create walls that act as barriers to the free flow of thoughts and feelings that invigorate your relationship. But when you open up to each other, the window between you allows you to know each other in unfiltered, intimate ways." This walls and windows analogy is particularly useful if your affair is emotional as well as sexual.

Significantly, betrayed partners often sense the relationship threat well before the sexual infidelity happens. For instance, Bret's wife stated that she never felt comfortable that her husband was working so closely with an attractive female colleague. She also said that Bret consistently devalued this opinion, and he agreed. Yet the wife was right. Becoming close to a female work colleague without setting clear boundaries was a bad call on Bret's part. He just didn't want to listen to his wife because he was having such a good time.

Generally speaking, emotional affairs feel much more potent than casual sex or recurring booty calls. For one thing, when you're emotionally connected to an affair partner (especially if she seems to be really into you), it becomes much more difficult to break things off, primarily because you care about her and don't want to hurt her. And if the sex was amazing, it can be even more difficult to pull away. That is perfectly natural and human; it's just not okay to use this connection as an excuse to stay in touch with your mistress. God's boundary for sex is a covenant relationship, not merely a connected friendship.

Making matters worse is that more damage is done to your primary relationship through an emotional affair than a purely sexual affair, because the more deeply you connect with the other woman, the more you move away from your mate, both emotionally and physically, no matter how much you may deny this swing. The windows slowly but steadily shift away from your spouse and you create walls, instead, with your secrets. You open windows toward your affair partner as the emotional intimacy increases. The longer you engage in the play, the banter, and the fun of the affair, the more powerful and ingrained this transference becomes. Over time, you find yourself turning to the other woman to work through your fears, meet your needs, help you resolve your confusing moments, and even share your spirituality. As you continually turn to her instead of your spouse for emotional intimacy, that connection feels increasingly meaningful—more so than your marriage at times.

Emotional affairs can be taken to an extreme. In fact, both of us have had clients who were living out more than one supposedly monogamous relationship simultaneously. They had full-fledged commitments to both women, maintaining two homes and two lives. Typically, these situations require a great deal of counseling (and legal wrangling) to resolve. In such cases, much more than this book is needed. More common, of course, is the man who feels deeply "in love" with two women at the same time: his wife and his affair partner. Though a bit less complicated than two totally separate households and wives, this scenario is especially painful for all involved. It will be explored further in chapter five.

Once you begin to confide in, rely on, and reach out to the other woman for emotional connection and understanding, especially if you're doing so in ways that you don't with your spouse, you start the journey away from your primary relationship.

This is true even if your "friendship" hasn't turned sexual, particularly if you find yourself lying or keeping secrets about it. Yep, that's the truth. Infidelity can involve "just" an emotional affair, which is the definition of this kind of intimate friendship, even if it isn't overtly romantic... yet. If you're in an emotionally charged relationship and you find yourself wondering when, exactly, you crossed the line, you might ask yourself the following:

- When did I start confiding more to the other woman than to my wife?
- When did I start talking to the other woman about problems in my marriage?
- When did I start keeping secrets from my spouse about the other woman, such as the amount of time we spend together, what we talk about, and what we do together?
- If my mate was an observer looking over my shoulder the whole time, at what point would she have said this friendship was hurting her?
- When did the friendship become tinged with sexual tension, causing the two of us to give each other special

glances across the room and to touch each other differently in private than in front of others?

All these questions boil down to the same thing: When did you make the other woman a priority over your spouse? Using Dr. Glass's terminology, when did the walls and windows begin to shift? The moment that happened is the moment your affair started. Sex or no sex, the first lie, the first secret, or the first time you prioritized the other woman over your mate was the beginning of your affair and your (possibly unconscious) shift away from your marriage and family life.

Consider Jesus' statements about adultery:

> "You have heard that it was said, 'Do not commit adultery.' But I tell you that anyone who looks at a woman lustfully has already committed adultery with her in his heart." (Matt. 5:27-28)

Ah, there's that heart thing again. A marriage is a sacred space beyond just the sexual. When you share intimate things with someone—personal, playful, financial, flirtatious, or spiritual things, to name just a few—that rightfully should be reserved for communion with only your wife, you are cheating.

Yeah, this doghouse stuff is really hard, huh?

But It Was Just a Webcam!

As our lives have moved increasingly into the virtual/digital arena, the once-clear line between sexual fidelity and cheating has, in many instances, become blurry for many men. Consider, for example, the following gray areas:

- Is chatting with a former girlfriend on social media sites like Facebook and Instagram a form of cheating?

- Is chatting with strangers on those same sites a form of cheating?
- What if you're chatting with women on hookup apps but not actually meeting them in person?
- Does sexting with a woman other than your wife qualify as sexual infidelity?
- Does viewing digital pornography qualify as cheating, and does it matter if there's masturbation in conjunction with that porn use?
- Does it matter how much porn you're looking at, how often you're viewing it, or if your spouse knows about it?
- What about engaging in mutual masturbation via webcam with a woman who lives thousands of miles away?
- Is webcam sex with a neighbor worse than webcam sex with a stranger?
- Is playing the video game Grand Theft Auto, which now offers sex with prostitutes as part of the action, or similarly sexualized video games, a form of cheating?

In today's increasingly digital world, the question that many men are asking is this: *Is live, in-person contact required for sexual infidelity, or does virtual sexual activity count equally?*

A few years ago, to answer this question, Doctors Jennifer Schneider, Charles Samenow, and Rob Weiss conducted a survey of women whose husbands were engaging in significant amounts of extramarital sexual activity, either online or in the real world. Probably the most important finding of their study was that when it comes to the negative effects of one partner having sex outside a supposedly monogamous relationship, tech-based and in-the-flesh sexuality are no different. The lying, the emotional distancing, and the pain of learning about the betrayal all feel exactly the same to the betrayed partner.

The results of this study confirm in many ways what we've already stated throughout this chapter. *It's not any specific sexual act that does the most damage to the betrayed partner and the relationship; instead, it's the constant lying, the emotional distancing, and the loss of relationship trust.* In fact, for most cheated-on partners the emotional betrayal associated with sexual infidelity is nearly always more painful and longer lasting than the physical betrayal. Thus, cheating encompasses both online and real-world sexual activity, as well as sexual and romantic activities that stop short of intercourse: everything from looking at porn to kissing another woman to something as simple as flirting.

Remember: Infidelity (cheating) is the breaking of trust that occurs when you keep intimate, meaningful secrets from your primary romantic partner. This definition squarely indicates the real issue for Christians—breaking a covenant commitment to love, honor, respect, and cherish your wife. Any of the types of cheating explored in this book (and any others you can come up with) clearly violate this standard.

Can You Hear Her?

Typically, men who cheat aren't fooling their partners as completely as they think. In other words, your wife may not have known exactly what you were up to, but she almost certainly knew that something was amiss. If so, you probably heard statements like the following:

- "I thought you said you'd be home on time tonight. Lately I never seem to know where you are or when you'll be home."
- "How am I supposed to plan for dinner and how we might spend our evenings?"
- "You seem distant. Is something wrong?"

- "Is there something going on that I don't know about? I have this feeling that you may be involved with someone else."
- "I feel uncomfortable when you go to Jason's house to play cards. Is that really what you're doing?"
- "You seem to spend more time with people from work than with me. Are you unhappy?"
- "We never talk anymore. Are you angry with me?"
- "We have so little sex these days. What's up with that?"

It's possible that your spouse even engaged in a bit of detective work, looking for facts that would confirm her suspicions. If so, she may have done things like the following:

- Looking at your bank account to check your spending.
- Driving past the place you were supposed to be (i.e., at the office working late) to see if that's really where you were.
- Going through your wallet to look for credit card receipts.
- Checking your phone for apps, texts, and anything else that might indicate what you've been doing.
- Checking the browser history on your computer to see what you've been up to online.

If your wife was, in your opinion, complaining or invading your privacy in these or other ways, it's likely that she was more in touch with your reality than you thought. She may have known that you were cheating while you were busily trying to convince yourself (and her) that you weren't. Her spirit knew.

A Bit of Homework…

At the end of each chapter we will pose several questions. Please consider these to be written homework assignments. They're designed to intensify your focus and make you think on a deeper level than if you were just reading along. We suggest buying a journal or a simple notebook in which you can write your answers. (You might also create a journal on your laptop.) We strongly urge you not to skip this work, because these aren't idle questions. Remember, the more effort you put into the process of healing, the more likely you are to repair and even to improve your relationship.

The questions and the work they invite aren't easy; in fact, they may be very painful. The word "repentance" actually means "to turn from," and true repentance is what God desires for you. The hardest part of healing from infidelity on the part of the betrayer is that it requires you to change, and change is difficult. The good news is that God has given you the capacity to change and to grow. The better news is that you don't have to do this tough work alone: God offers help every moment and step of the way.

Start by being brutally honest with yourself and in your answers. (To ensure honesty, this written work is best kept private, so take care to store it safely.) Be courageous and tell yourself and God the truth.

Questions for Reflection

1. Before you read this chapter, did you believe that you had cheated on your significant other? After reading this chapter, do you think otherwise? Do you believe that your cheating may have been more extensive than you initially thought?

2. Do you feel bad about your extramarital sexual activity (beyond the fact that you got caught)? Please don't answer yes simply because that's the Christian thing to do. Do you feel bad about the secrets and lies that surrounded that behavior? Which do you feel worse about, the behavior or the lying? Which do you think your significant other feels worse about?

3. In what ways has your lack of sexual and romantic integrity affected other aspects of your life? How do you feel about that? Do you see any obvious (heart) changes that you could make to put your life back into alignment? If so, what are they?

4. Write a paragraph to God about your honest thoughts and feelings. If you're willing, ask for God's help to accept your stint in the doghouse with humility. If you're not ready for that step, consider talking with God about your unwillingness. God already knows the state of your heart and welcomes your honesty (especially considering your deep dishonesty for however long). Even that response is a redemptive start!

CHAPTER TWO

WELL, OKAY, I GUESS YOU COULD CALL IT CHEATING

"There is no point in using the word 'impossible' to describe something that has clearly happened."
—Douglas Adams, *Dirk Gently's Holistic Detective Agency*

Denial is a Beautiful Thing, Until It Isn't

Franklin is a forty-year-old married father of two teenage daughters. Ten years ago, he discovered online pornography. His sex life with his wife had diminished significantly after their daughters were born, so porn seemed like a great alternative. When feeling horny, he didn't have to bug his harried wife for sex anymore. Instead, he could go online for fifteen or twenty minutes, find some hot pics or videos, and take care of things on his own. He also began to enjoy chatting up random women on dating websites, social media, and "adult friend-finder" apps. If these women were open to mutual masturbation via webcam that was even better. But he never met with or had sex with another woman in person. Thus, in his mind, he never cheated.

A few months ago, Franklin's wife uncovered his secret world of online activities when she borrowed his phone and found the apps and webcam videos on it. She was incredibly angry and accused Franklin of serial infidelity. He, however, insisted that he had never cheated because all he'd ever done was look at porn and chat online. "It's no different than my dad looking at Playboy when I was a kid," he argued. "So why are you giving me such a hard time?"

It's no surprise that his wife disagreed with that assessment. She said, "You may think that it's the same as a magazine or video back in the day, but it sure doesn't feel that way to me. This isn't something that sits in a drawer next to our bed or in the closet. This is content that our children could find, that I have seen you using. And not just occasionally, either. It would be one thing if we had an amazing and intimate sex life, but we don't. In fact, you rarely approach or encourage me to have sex. So how am I supposed to feel? I mean, you have no problem having sex with these 'paper dolls' or whatever they are to you, but what about me? How is this not like an affair if I feel just as left out and alone? Besides, even if this is just entertainment for you, how come you don't seem to care how it makes me feel? Since when did my feelings come second to your sex play? And then you criticize our daughters for how they dress or stand up and pray in church! You hypocrite!"

Often, one of the most difficult aspects of helping a guy who's in trouble for cheating is getting him to view infidelity for what is. Even after reading the first chapter of this book, which clearly defines infidelity, you might not acknowledge what you've done as cheating, or you still might not understand why your significant other won't just accept what has happened, including "her part" in it. You may wonder why she won't immediately forgive you (after all, you've said you're sorry) and perhaps even understand why you did it.

So, if you're like most cheating men, you'll rationalize, minimize, and justify your sex play—blaming everyone and everything but yourself for your actions and the doghouse in which you now find yourself. Perhaps you've thought or said things like the following:

- "Every guy wants to have sex with other women. And when the opportunity arises, he acts on it, especially if he probably won't get caught."
- "If my job wasn't so stressful, I wouldn't need the release that porn gives me."
- "I'm only sexting and flirting. Where's the harm in that?
- I don't meet up with any of these women in person. It's just a game to me."
- "My dad looked at porn and went to strip clubs, and it wasn't a big deal. Well, I have webcam chats and virtual sex. What's the difference?"
- "If my wife hadn't gained so much weight and stopped enjoying sex, I wouldn't have even thought about going elsewhere."
- "If the police had been out chasing real criminals, I wouldn't have gotten caught in that prostitution sting. Damn cops!" (Yes, we know Christian men cuss, too.)
- "Monogamy means no romantic connections, like no kissing, no cuddling, and no getting attached. A lap dance in a strip club is hardly a romantic connection. It's just what guys do for fun."

In the therapy business, we have a name for this type of reasoning: We call it *denial*. From a psychotherapy perspective, denial is a series of internal lies and deceits that people tell themselves to make their questionable behavior seem okay. Typically, each self-deception is supported by one or more rationalizations, with each rationalization bolstered by still more falsehoods. And so it goes.

When viewed from a distance, denial is about as structurally sound as a house of cards in a stiff breeze, yet most cheaters behave as if they're living in an impenetrable bomb shelter. (Until they find themselves in the doghouse.) Without doubt, an impartial observer could easily see through the smokescreen, but most unfaithful men either cannot or will not, choosing instead to ignore the seriousness and potential consequences of their actions so they can comfortably carry on with their cheating. And this willful ignorance can go on for years—usually continuing until their infidelity is discovered, and often beyond that.

If Christian men allow themselves to consider the negative at all, they are likely to feel guilt and shame for their behavior. But those guilty feelings are temporary—uncomfortable naggings that only fleetingly penetrate past the more powerful feeling of denial. As a result, your guilt and shame over your cheating actually build higher walls between you and your spouse, rather than leading to heart and behavior change.

The Reality About Paid Sex and Porn

Men who use porn and/or paid webcam shows tend to see idealized women's body parts and graphic, hyper-intense sexual acts, but not much else. What they tend to *not* notice is that the women depicted are in fact real people, with real thoughts and feelings. Moreover, many of these women have life histories filled with profound abuse, neglect, poverty, and addiction—which, by the way, is what landed them in the sex industry in the first place.

If you're a consumer of porn, strip clubs, webcam sex, escorts, and the like, you need to understand that the women involved are probably not enjoying themselves as much as you might think. In all likelihood, these women are "performing sex" to pay for childcare, make the rent, or feed a drug habit. They might also be re-enacting painful early-life trauma and abuse. In short, these are typically women who have very few genuine survival options other than being a sex worker (for far too many reasons to review here). Trust us, this is almost certainly not fun and games for them; it's difficult, painful work with little long-term reward.

Our point is that even though porn and other pay-to-play sex industry activities may look great to you as a consumer, they're not nearly as much fun for the sex workers. In fact, the sex you see tends to feel more demeaning and abusive to them than pleasurable. We venture to say that probably no woman grew up dreaming of being a porn star or thinks this is her perfect job. The reality of the industry is far from "consensual" in the most complete sense of the word. Beyond those hot body parts, there may well be a woman who is struggling to simply survive.

Standard-Issue Denial

The most common type of denial, used by almost every man who cheats, is built on the following lie: *What she doesn't know can't hurt her.* Frankly, we're amazed by the fact that cheating men are almost always able to convince themselves that this statement is true. *It isn't!* Even though your spouse may have had no idea that you were sleeping around, it's almost certain that she felt and experienced some degree of emotional and even physical distancing on your part. Sadly, she may have blamed herself for this rift, and wondered what she had done to create it.

Your Kids Are Hurting, Too!

Children also notice emotional distancing in their caregivers. They wonder why Daddy seems so uninterested in them, why he's not as fun and available as he used to be, and why he and Mommy don't hug all the time like they once did. *And children are even more likely than spouses to internalize the blame for this divide.* Despite their young age, kids know that something is wrong, but they mistakenly think it's somehow their fault. To young kids, parents are perfect, so if something goes wrong they assume that it must be their fault. As the days pass, children of all ages start to feel less important, less special, and less wanted, which does a pretty serious number on their self-esteem. Therefore, your rationalization that "even if I was hurtful to my wife, at least I never let it affect the kids" is just smoke and mirrors.

We know that you really don't want to think about this aspect of your situation. But it's true, and there's no sense in pretending that it isn't. When you cheat, you hurt your kids as much as you hurt your spouse, and sometimes more.

In our work with adults who have experienced infidelity, both as the betrayer and as the betrayed partner, many grew up in a home with some kind of cheating. Is that legacy what you want for your kids?

In therapy sessions, regardless of the nature of the lies that our unfaithful male clients tell themselves (and us) to justify their sexual infidelity, we generally respond with one very simple question, which we now pose to you: *If your behavior wasn't cheating, then why were you keeping it a secret from your wife?*

If you're like most cheating men, you have an easy answer for this: "I didn't want to upset her or cause her any pain." But were you really trying to protect your mate from pain, or were you more focused on protecting yourself from being found out so you could continue doing whatever you wanted with whomever you wanted?

The correct answer to this question, in case you're wondering, is that you were almost assuredly trying to protect yourself (and your cheating), not your spouse.

Occasionally, when an unfaithful man seems especially self-focused and determined to believe his own lies, no matter how ridiculous they sound to an impartial observer (i.e., us), we suggest that his sexual behavior might be perfectly fine within the boundaries of his relationship if only his wife knew about his actions up front and agreed that they were okay. We then suggest that if he and his spouse can mutually agree, without coercion of any sort, that certain extramarital sexual behaviors are acceptable, then so be it. In such cases, he can continue in good conscience with what he's doing.

Picture the following: On your way out the door you say, "Honey, I've been feeling sexually deprived lately. Actually, I've been feeling this way ever since the kids came along. So instead of going to that work conference I told you about, I'm going to buy some booze and cocaine, hire a couple of sex workers, and party in a hotel all weekend. You can reach me by cell if you need me."

Guess what? In all our years as therapists we have never, not even once, had a cheating client take us up on our suggestion to be open and forthright with his partner. (Even if the couple weren't Christian or religious in any other way.) Nor have we ever expected that to happen. And why would we? Practically speaking, if any of these clients was in a relationship in which he thought his spouse would accept his extracurricular sexual activities, he'd surely have broached the topic with her already. And our guess, based on the fact that you're reading this book, is that you are no different. If you thought that your significant other would be okay with your sextracurricular activity, you'd have told her about it up front, and you wouldn't be in the doghouse.

Spiritually speaking, the answer is obvious. Deep down, as a Christian, you know that your sexcapades are out of bounds. You haven't so fully lost yourself that you think anything goes as long as it's out in the open with your wife. A part of you, however small or deeply buried, gets the concepts of the heart and the sanctity of a covenant relationship. A part of you understands that God's truth about the makeup of a healthy and fulfilling relationship is different from the world's. You just wish you could somehow get around that constricting boundary and do what you want without impunity.

"Out There" Activity

Lots of guys have an embarrassing or shame-inducing interest in "out there" sexual activity like kink (bondage and discipline, sadomasochism, feet, leather, and the like) and/or sex with other men or transgender people. And many would prefer that their mate not know about these interests out of fear that she might reject them. So, they secretly act out their desires, especially online, without their spouse's knowledge. To make this okay, they tell themselves, *Looking at BDSM porn or getting a spanking from a dominatrix isn't cheating because nobody actually touches me. And I'm just online, so it's not a big deal. It's just safe exploration. So what if I masturbate immediately after the spanking?* Or maybe they tell themselves, *Messing around with another guy in the steam room at the gym is just messing around, not cheating. If I was with a woman, that would be cheating, but guys don't count.*

If you're denying the fact that you've cheated with thoughts like these, we suggest you remember that infidelity is as much about lying and keeping secrets as it is about any actual sex act.

An important and admittedly scary part of your owning your stuff is to come clean eventually with your significant other about your hidden sexual interests and activities. Amazingly, that vulnerable conversation will almost certainly bring you closer over time instead of pushing you apart (as you might have feared). The worst thing you can do is continue to engage in extramarital sexual activity, lie, and keep secrets.

Beyond Denial: The Real Reasons You Cheat

As discussed above, most men who cheat on their intimate partners justify their behavior with all sorts of ridiculous excuses, few of which hold up in the cold light of day. Sadly, even when these lies are debunked, plenty of men continue cheating. This, of course, raises the following questions: Why did you really start cheating? Why did you continue to do so even in the face of profoundly unwanted potential consequences like divorce, loss of parental contact, loss of social standing, and more? And why did you keep cheating when a part of you knew it violated your covenant with God as well as with your wife?

Generally, when you engage in sexual infidelity, you do so for one or more of the following (relatively unflattering) reasons:

- **Insecurity.** You feel too old (or too young), not handsome enough, not rich enough, not smart enough, or not powerful enough. As a result, you seek validation from women other than your mate, using their spark of interest to feel wanted, desired, and worthy. You use extramarital sex to bolster your flagging ego and feel better about yourself.
- **Unfettered impulse.** You never thought much about cheating until buxom Brenda hit on you at the office party, letting you know she was up for "it" whenever and wherever. Without even thinking about what your behavior might do to your primary relationship, you went for it.
- **Psychological trauma.** You are re-enacting and/or latently responding to unresolved childhood traumas: neglect, emotional abuse, physical abuse, or sexual abuse. Essentially, your childhood and adolescent wounds have created intimacy issues that leave you unable and/or unwilling to fully commit to one person. You might also be using the excitement and distraction of sexual infidelity to soothe the pain of these old, unhealed wounds.
- **Terminal uniqueness.** You feel deserving of something special that is just for you: a prostitute, a few hours with pornography, an emotional affair, a sexual affair, etc. You

convince yourself that you are "put upon" in some way by the people in your life, and you use this to justify your infidelity.

- **Lack of male social support.** You have undervalued your need for supportive friendships with other men, and you expect your social and emotional needs to be met entirely by your wife. When she inevitably fails in that duty, you look elsewhere.
- **Biology.** You believe it's a man's evolutionary right or imperative to spread his seed as widely as possible. Or maybe you believed that in your promiscuous days before you became a Christian, and you haven't fully stopped that dogging around. Either way, acting on this belief conflicts with your commitment to monogamy and breaches relationship trust, which is why you're now in the doghouse.
- **Unrealistic expectations.** You believe that your partner should meet your every whim and desire, sexual and otherwise, 24/7, regardless of how she's feeling at any particular moment. You fail to understand that she has a life of her own, with thoughts and feelings and needs that don't always involve you. When your expectations aren't met, you seek external fulfillment.
- **It's over, version 1.** You want to end your current relationship. However, instead of just telling your significant other that you're unhappy and want to break things off, you cheat and force her to take this unpleasant step herself. This might seem like the easy way out, but it's not. (If you're reading this book, this probably doesn't apply to you.)
- **It's over, version 2.** You want to end your current relationship. However, you don't want to leave until you've got another relationship lined up. You set the stage for your next relationship while you're still in the first one—only you do this without letting your current partner know

that she's being used and strung along in this way. (Once again, if you're reading this book, this probably doesn't apply to you.)
- **Limerence.** You don't grasp the difference between romantic intensity and long-term love. You fail to understand that in healthy long-term relationships the rush of early romance (limerence) is replaced over time with less intense but ultimately more meaningful forms of connection. To be honest, you are relationally immature.
- **Co-occurring issues.** Maybe you have an ongoing problem with alcohol and/or drugs that affects your decision making, which results in regrettable sexual decisions. Or maybe you have a problem like sexual addiction, which means that you compulsively engage in sexual fantasies and activities to numb out and avoid life. (This desire for escape is also why alcoholics drink, drug addicts get high, and compulsive gamblers place bets.)
- **Putting yourself first.** Your primary consideration is for yourself and yourself alone. You can therefore lie and keep secrets without remorse or regret as long as it gets you what you want. It's possible that you never intended to be monogamous. Rather than seeing your vow of monogamy as a sacrifice made to and for your relationship, you view it as something to be avoided and worked around. Perhaps you voiced that marriage vow simply because your wife is a Christian and wanted a traditional, faith-based wedding ceremony. You never really bought into the monogamy part.

There is a small amount of scientific evidence suggesting that certain people may be genetically predisposed toward infidelity. This school of thought suggests a small number of men and women are genetically predisposed to produce and/or process various pleasure-related neurochemicals in slightly atypical ways that make cheating more likely. So now you might be thinking about taking this book over to your wife, waving it in her face, and saying, "See, it's not my fault. Some guys are genetically predisposed to cheat."

A strong suggestion here: Don't do that! That's the sort of thing that will alienate your spouse and cause her to become very, very angry. You might never get out of the doghouse, and frankly that might be the best place for you to stay.

Anyway, you are probably *not* genetically predisposed toward infidelity. Most likely, you behaved the way you did for one or more of the reasons listed above. And even if a genetic predisposition did play into your behavior, you don't get a free pass. After all, a correlation between certain genetic variations and promiscuity doesn't mean that these variations automatically and inherently lead to sexual infidelity. For an analogy, consider alcohol. Plenty of people are genetically predisposed toward alcoholism, but only a small percentage become alcoholic because many other factors are in play (like environment, willpower, life experience, and resiliency to turmoil). The same is true with a genetic predisposition toward promiscuity. Other factors are in play, including your vow and view of monogamy. Therefore, regardless of your genetics, you maintain free will when it comes to sexual behavior. You always have a choice.

> Note: Your significant other doesn't really care why you cheated (even if she asks). What she cares about is that you hurt her (and the rest of your family) by doing it. From her perspective, as well as from the perspective of saving your relationship, whether you are genetically predisposed toward infidelity or just a strongly self-focused person who didn't care much for monogamy doesn't matter. What matters is what you are going to do in the future—what kind of man, husband, friend, parent, and partner you are going to be moving forward.

For most men there's no single factor that drives the decision to cheat. It's possible that the reasons you cheated aren't listed above. It's also possible that your reasons for cheating evolved over time, as your life circumstances changed. Regardless of your reasons for cheating, you didn't have to do it. You had many other options: seeking couple's therapy, taking up golf, being open and honest with your wife and working to improve the relationship, or even separating and/or getting divorced. There are always choices that don't involve degrading and potentially ruining your integrity and the life that you and your spouse have created. Nevertheless, knowing why you cheated can be helpful in terms of not repeating this behavior in the future.

Special Circumstances

Over the years we have come to realize that there are occasionally legitimate reasons for a man wanting to be sexual outside his primary relationship, although that doesn't mean it's okay for him to pursue that desire. We nevertheless believe that it's helpful to recognize situations like the following:

- Your partner has profound physical problems that prevent her from having, desiring, and/or enjoying sex.
- Your partner consistently refuses to have sex or is reviled by the experience of sex, and she isn't willing to work on the underlying psychological cause(s) of her aversion.
- You and your partner are separated for long periods because of career demands or other commitments.

These are real-life, not-all-that-unusual circumstances that can occur either temporarily or long-term. To be sure, these are painful and difficult situations. Equally for certain, they deserve honest and vulnerable conversations between you and your wife. If she isn't psychologically capable of such a conversation, you should at least consult with a trusted therapist and a spiritual advisor, which is likely a necessary step anyway.

Consider Sam and Mary. After Mary was paralyzed from the neck down in a diving accident, she obviously was unable to perform sexually, and she was no longer interested in anything sexual. For Sam, of course, this was a disappointment.

Because they loved each other very much and had no interest in ending their marriage, they were able to agree on certain sexual boundaries. For instance, Sam was free to masturbate as long as it didn't involve pornography or fantasy other than about their shared sexual activity. As they adjusted to their new normal, Mary came to enjoy seeing Sam masturbate and hearing how he was imagining being sexual with her. This vulnerability sparked a bit of sexual desire for Mary. Though she was never able to bodily participate in sex, she got significant pleasure from Sam's tender and sensual massages. They remained committed to monogamy, got creative, and discovered unique ways to share sexual energy. Two decades later, they are still happily married.

Consider also the case of Jack, who was married to a woman who became chronically mentally ill to the point where she needed to be institutionalized. Jack's insurance paid for her care and treatment, and he took seriously his vows to love her "in sickness and in health." He never considered divorce. But he also knew that his wife would never again be well enough for healthy and enjoyable physical intimacy. In fact, her psychiatrist and primary therapist believed she was too fragile for a discussion of their relationship and Jack's loneliness, much less one about his sexual needs.

This scenario is even more difficult than Sam and Mary's. Jack had no reasonable hope that his wife could be a participating life partner. She would likely spend the rest of her days in the institution, which was the only place that could provide the safety and care she needed. Jack also chose monogamous masturbation, and he took care to guard his heart against sexual temptation. He also fostered healthy and deep emotional relationships with other Christian men, who provided safe companionship and support.

Life happens, and circumstances change. Covenant marriage is just that—a covenant that isn't justifiably broken just because life gets hard. Integrity and whole-heartedness don't depend on pleasant life situations. Sometimes you have a "thorn in the flesh" like the apostle Paul (2 Cor. 12:7-10). Despite your repeated prayers, it doesn't go away. Our prayer is that, like Paul, you will find that "[God's] grace is sufficient for you, for [your] power is made perfect in weakness."

The Man in the Mirror

Maybe you are now ready to accept the reality that you cheated, that your actions caused others (whom you claim to love) actual harm, and that your choice to cheat was one of your poorest decisions. If so, it's time to take an objective look in the mirror. But be warned: You might not like what you see. Instead of the bright, shiny, smiling, trustworthy, loving man you're hoping for, you are likely to see the following:

- **Secrets and lies.** You weren't open about your sextracurricular activities. When you were caught in a lie or a secret, you attempted to cover it up with still more lies and secrets. And you seemed not to care how much this upset your significant other.
- **Manipulation.** You tried to hide your behavior by convincing your spouse to believe all sorts of lame and unlikely excuses. You were incredibly persistent with this strategy. You kept at it until she wore down and gave in. You tried to make her believe that she was the one with a problem (e.g., insecurity, imagining things).
- **Broken promises.** You promised your wife that you would be more present in your relationship. And you even followed through for a few days or weeks. But eventually you pulled away again and returned to the allure of illicit sexual behavior.

- **Mood swings.** Sometimes you were extremely loving and happy in your primary relationship. Unfortunately, these interludes were followed by periods of irritability and disconnection. If questioned, you blamed your mood swings on the actions of others or events beyond your control.
- **Emotional detachment.** You were more involved with affair partners, prostitutes, pornography, sexting, chat rooms, hookup apps, and similar sextracurricular activities than with your spouse.
- **Financial issues.** Extramarital sex costs money. Even if you have a job that pays well, you may have found yourself living on the edge financially. Perhaps you were late paying bills, or you ignored your financial obligations altogether. Meanwhile, you told your partner blatant lies about your expenditures to conceal your infidelity.
- **Damaged reputation.** Because your sexual activities were not as secret as you would have liked or thought, you lost standing with neighbors, coworkers, bosses, subordinates, and even friends.
- **Emotional withdrawal.** You avoided talking about problems in your relationship because you didn't want to even consider changing your behavior. Your consistent reaction to any concern expressed by your significant other was anger, denial, defensiveness, and/or blaming. You seemed not to care how much this upset her.
- **Damaged health and self-esteem.** You may have contracted a sexually transmitted disease or some other communicable infection. You may also have been arrested, fired, or otherwise disciplined. If so, your health and self-image has suffered.
- **Spiritual disconnection.** As much as you convinced yourself otherwise, your cheating impaired you spiritually. Your guilt and shame distanced you from God and

Christian others, including your wife. You may have stopped praying, reading scripture, or being active in church because you felt like a hypocrite. Even Christian music became painful, and you turned it off.

It's not a pretty picture, is it? But that's what you'll see when you look honestly at your behavior. No, of course you never intended to do things like the following:

- Harm your primary relationship.
- Alienate your family.
- Ignore your kids.
- Potentially expose your children to sexual images and information.
- Risk your career and social standing.
- Blame your bad behavior on people you love.
- Mangle your finances.
- Fight constantly with your significant other.
- Fill yourself with shame, self-hatred, and remorse.
- Push the self-destruct button on everything that matters most to you.
- Weaken your spiritual connection with God.

Nevertheless, you now find yourself dealing with these or similar circumstances, arriving there incrementally (or maybe very quickly). What initially seemed like a manageable situation spiraled downward into destruction.

As your attempts at self-protection increased, you became less and less able (and less willing) to see the connection between your increasing personal problems and your sexual behavior. You grew increasingly deaf to the complaints, concerns, and criticisms of those around you—even those you professed to love. You correspondingly devalued and dismissed (and/or blamed) those who tried to point out the problem. You wanted to have your cake and eat it, too, so you opted for offense as your best defense. You accused (in your head or aloud) your betrayed partner of nagging, lacking trust, being prudish and restrictive, failing to understand you, and just plain asking for too much. And you did this not because you truly don't care, but to justify and protect your infidelity.

What you forgot, however, was the importance of safeguarding hearth and home and your past promise of fidelity. In case you haven't figured it out by now, those things, much more than your extracurricular sexual exploits, are the most important facets of your life.

Questions for Reflection

1. How often did your cheating occur, and why? Do you know what might have triggered it?

2. How did you justify your behavior to yourself? How did you justify your behavior to others who knew about or suspected it?

3. Do you think your spouse had a sense that something was amiss even before she learned about your cheating? If so, for how long? And what lies did you tell her to throw her off the track?

CHAPTER THREE

HOW WOMEN (AND MEN) VIEW RELATIONSHIPS AND BETRAYAL

> "We mistakenly assume that if our partners love us they will react and behave in certain ways—the ways we react and behave when we love someone."
> —John Gray, *Men Are from Mars, Women Are from Venus*

When your wife found out about your cheating (or some of your cheating, anyway), her first reaction was probably something like utter rage, or at least a whole world of hurt. And she's probably still quite reactive, regardless of how many days, weeks, or months it's been since her discovery. To you, this probably seems extreme, especially if your behavior was purely sexual with little to no emotional or psychological connection. You might think, *Sure, I violated my vow of monogamy, but I told her it didn't mean anything and I'm sorry. So now it's time for her to let it go and get back to normal. Right?*

Nevertheless, she is still extremely angry and upset. As mentioned earlier, her reaction is because men and women view sex and relationships in very different ways. Men are typically able to separate and compartmentalize sex and intimate connections, whereas women typically are not. For you, as a man, sex is sex and relationships are relationships, and the two things don't necessarily overlap. With your spouse you absolutely have (or had) an intertwined sexual and emotional attraction and connection. With your casual sex partners and quickie affairs, whether online or in-person, you may or may not have felt that way. And if you didn't, that probably made it very easy for you to separate your cheating from your primary relationship. Except for the pesky guilt, you viewed your extracurricular sexual activity as a perfectly normal, enjoyable, and harmless activity—like playing on the company softball team or grabbing a beer with the guys.

However, as you're now finding out, this isn't a thought process that your spouse understands or believes, because women in committed relationships are typically much less able than men to separate and compartmentalize sex and emotional connection.

For evidence of this male-female dichotomy, consider the results of a well-known secular study (Chivers et al., 2004) in which men and women were shown videos of two men having sex and two women having sex. The male test subjects' responses were highly specific by sexual orientation. Straight guys were turned on only by the videos of women, and gay guys were turned on only by the videos of men. Meanwhile, two-thirds of the women, regardless of their sexual orientation, were aroused by both male and female stimuli—in particular, the videos that displayed or at least hinted at an emotional and psychological connection between the partners. And this research is hardly an outlier. Numerous other studies have produced similar results, confirming that in general women are attracted to and turned on by emotional intimacy (especially in committed relationships), whereas men are turned on by body parts and sex acts.

For women, therefore, emotional connection and sexual arousal are deeply intertwined. That's why your significant other is behaving the way she's behaving. When you cheated, regardless of how the act made you feel or what it meant to you, you wounded your mate not just sexually, but emotionally.

Exacerbating matters is the fact that your wife probably sees your betrayal in a holistic way, looking at how your behavior affects her entire life. So instead of thinking, *You had sex with another woman and I'm really angry about that*, she's probably thinking something like, *It's not just me that you've betrayed; it's our children, our home, our community, and our church.* She is probably also thinking (if not saying) things like, *If you lied to me about your sex life, then what else have you been lying about? Sexual faithfulness is our most sacred vow! How can I believe anything you say ever again or anything you've ever said so far?* Basically, when you cheat on your spouse, she sees a much bigger picture than just the sex. Even though your behavior may seem inconsequential to you, your significant other will likely view it as all-encompassing.

The Neurochemistry of Love

The powerful initial romantic/sexual interest that we sometimes feel (known as limerence) is usually enough to keep us with another person long enough to decide if our attraction extends beyond physical appearance. If there is more to the connection, then we may decide to stick around, and we develop emotional intimacy in addition to sexual attraction. In all likelihood, this is what happened with your mate. You thought she was attractive, you asked her out, you realized that you also liked her as a person, and the two of you built a meaningful life together. Or maybe you felt an early, strong sexual attraction or even had sex with her right away; and then, a few days or weeks later, you realized there was something beyond just a hot attraction, so you went back for more, this time looking for a deeper relationship.

Inside your brain this process is both simple and traceable. In fact, researchers, using functional magnetic resonance imaging (fMRI) scans, can easily watch what happens in your brain as you meet, like, and eventually love another person. Basically, fMRI scans are used to monitor activity in various regions of the brain in response to specific stimuli. When one portion of the brain is activated—by a thought, an emotion, a movement, or anything else— blood flow to and within that area increases, and fMRI scans clearly depict this response.

One study (Cacioppo et al., 2012) analyzed the results of twenty separate fMRI trials looking at brain reactivity in response to physical attraction, sexual arousal, and long-term love. After pooling data, scientists were able to map the ways in which sexual desire and long-term love stimulate the brain. The two main findings were as follows:

- Sexual desire and long-term love both stimulate the striatum, the area of the brain that includes the nucleus accumbens (which is often referred to as the rewards center). This means that both sexual attraction and lasting love create the experience of pleasure.
- Long-term love (but *not* sexual desire) also stimulates the insula, the area of the brain associated with motivation. Essentially, the insula gives value to pleasurable and/or life-sustaining activities to make sure we continue to engage in them. This means lasting love has an inherent neurobiological value that sexual attraction does not. (Is God's design cool, or what?)

In short, your brain's rewards center is responsible for initial attraction and sexual desire, whereas the value center is responsible for transforming that desire into long-term love.

Significantly, the rewards center is also the area of the brain most closely associated with the formation of addiction. In fact, addictive substances and activities thoroughly stimulate this segment of the brain. As such, it's hardly surprising that some people (i.e., cheaters) might repeatedly pursue the initial and highly stimulating limerence stage of relationships. After all, limerence produces the same high (the same basic neurobiological stimulation) as cocaine, heroin, alcohol, chocolate, nicotine, and the like, primarily through the release of dopamine, adrenaline, oxytocin, serotonin, and a few other pleasure-inducing neurochemicals.

We wouldn't be at all surprised if you told us that you sometimes felt high when you were chasing other women. Most men who cheat do at times feel this way, as do the women who cheat. The difference between the sexes is that men are usually able to separate this neurochemical rush from their sense of emotional attachment, whereas women typically cannot. This is why a handjob from a stranger at a party (perhaps fueled by too much to drink) can mean nothing to you and everything to your spouse.

Whether you fully understand the neuroscience discussed above isn't important. What matters is your understanding that in most men the neurochemical response to casual cheating is centered in the brain's rewards center, with little or no long-term value attached. In other words, men think about how good sex will feel, and that's about it. It's entirely possible that you felt no emotional connection at all to the woman or women with whom you cheated. However, your wife neither thinks nor operates in this fashion. For her, sex and emotional connection are one and the same. Thus, you shouldn't expect her to "get over it" as easily as you think she ought to.

But don't bother trying to explain this to her as a way of helping her understand that she shouldn't be as angry with you as she appears to be. That won't alleviate her pain or stop her from being angry. In fact, it might just infuriate her even more. There is no excuse, biological or otherwise, for your cheating, and a neurochemistry lesson will feel like (and is) a justification jazzed up with some medical jargon. The main reason we've included this information is to help you understand why you and your spouse view your "meaningless" sex so differently.

Or Versus And

For a moment, let's set aside a Christian values-based perspective and look at sexual desire through a purely biological lens. It's probably not a surprise for you to learn that male sexual desire is driven more by physiological than psychological factors. This is why porn sites created for male users feature sexual body parts and/or overt sexual acts and not much else. In male-oriented porn, there's rarely a storyline, kissing, foreplay, or any romantic interaction. Men don't see a real person on the receiving end of whatever is being inserted. For the unbridled male brain, it's just sex, sex, and more sex. Even pornographic "literature" written for a male audience tends to focus much more on body parts and sexual acts than on the development of relationships and feelings.

Women operate differently. Open a romance novel or tune in to *True Blood*, the *Twilight* movies, and other female-oriented romance and erotica, and you'll see this rather clearly. In these stories, be they written or visual, you'll find very little in the way of purely objectified, non-relational sex. Instead, you get a bunch of broad-chested, square-jawed, deep-voiced bad boys turning into goo whenever they spot the story's heroine. Think *Fifty Shades of Grey*. (Yes, for wives who are reading, a large percentage of Christians reported reading *Fifty Shades* or seeing the movie.) While male-oriented pornography focuses on a woman's erogenous areas (and maybe the man's huge penis penetrating her in some way), erotica for women focuses on how the man makes her feel and, perhaps more important, how *she* makes *him* feel. So, yet again, women tend to be more turned on by emotional connection than by body parts and sex acts.

One easy way to think about this dichotomy involves *or* versus *and*. For men, sexual arousal is a matter of *or*. For instance, a guy sees a woman with beautiful breasts *or* a nice butt *or* sexy legs *or* whatever—pretty much anything at all that seems even remotely sexual to him—and he gets turned on. Certainly men can be turned on by a nice personality as well, but more often they're turned on by specific body parts. Men do not need to be *in love* to enjoy sex. In fact, most guys don't even need to be *in like*. They just have to be turned on.

Meanwhile, the process of sexual arousal in women is quite different. It's much more difficult to get a woman interested in sex because, for her, it's not a matter of *or*, it's a matter of *and*. Women want a deep voice *and* a hairy chest *and* big biceps *and* a good job *and* a sense of humor *and* the desire to fix up a house together *and* kindness *and* a whole bunch of other stuff.

This very important male-female difference is expounded on by secular researchers Ogi Ogas and Sai Gaddam (2011) as follows:

> When contemplating sex with a man, a woman has to consider the long-term. This consideration may not even be conscious, but rather is part of the unconscious software that has evolved to protect women over hundreds of thousands of years. Sex could commit a woman to a substantial, life-altering investment: pregnancy, nursing, and more than a decade of child-raising. These commitments require enormous time, resources, and energy. Sex with the wrong guy could lead to many unpleasant outcomes.... A woman's sexual desire must be filtered through a careful appraisal of these potential risks.

Ogas and Gaddam call this feminine need to thoroughly vet a potential partner's physical and character traits before becoming both physically and psychologically turned on "Miss Marple," referring to novelist Agatha's Christie's crusty yet astute female detective. They note that a woman's internal Miss Marple is not willing to approve sexual arousal until multiple conditions are met. Miss Marple says, "Sure, he's cute, but does he have a good job? Does he share my faith? Is he interested in marriage? Does he have a history of cheating? Is he a heavy drinker? Has he ever been abusive?" All this must be considered before a woman says yes to sex.

> Note: Disinhibiting substances (like alcohol) can short-circuit a woman's inner Miss Marple. This is why men typically find it easier to hook up with women who've had a few drinks. Essentially, booze puts to sleep the part of a woman's brain that says no to sex unless her internal conditions are met.

In case you're wondering, men do not have such an inner detective. As a result, male sexual arousal typically looks something like this: *Wow, would you look at that! That is hot! I wonder what it would be like to have sex with that. I'm going for it!*

Interestingly, female sexual arousal starts out the same way, though it quickly takes a different path: *Wow, would you look at that! That is hot! I wonder if he has a good job. His hands are soft. I bet he's gentle. But, of course, none of that matters because I'm already in a relationship and I don't want to hurt my husband, my kids, or any other aspect of my life. I'll just forget about this and move on.*

This dichotomy is why your hot, meaningless sexual hookup is relatively easy for you to dismiss, but your wife can't seem to let it go. She just doesn't think the way you do. In her mind, the only reasons for you to have sex outside your marriage are the following:

- You care about the other woman as much as or more than you care about her.
- She is somehow not making you happy, so you're looking for fulfillment elsewhere.

Hence, you are now faced with her seemingly irrational and disproportionate surge of fear, rage, and emotionally unpredictable behavior, even though, from your perspective, all you did was get a lap dance from a stripper.

> Note: Just because men are easily turned on doesn't mean they have to act on that feeling. And most guys

don't. So even though men may be genetically programmed to want sex with as many women as possible, that's not how they generally behave. Instead, they think through the process and weigh the pros and cons before making a decision. As such, a happily married man might ideally think, *Gee, this woman is very hot, but she's also a neighbor and a good friend of my wife. Besides, sex outside my marriage is totally out of bounds. So, as great as she looks—and boy, she does look great—I'm going to shut the door on lusting after her.* Unfortunately, that sort of thinking is sometimes discarded for momentary gratification, as you well know.

Again, let us remind you of God's invitation to integrity. You are endowed with free will, and if you're wise, you will hone that freedom by the discipline of using it regularly in a positive way. This is part of your own healing work and crucial to your release from the doghouse.

The Shock of Betrayal

When cheating is discovered, the betrayed partner is nearly always emotionally traumatized. Even if she suspected that something was amiss in the relationship before her discovery, she's blown away when she officially learns the truth. In fact, research shows that wives who learn about their husbands' cheating typically experience stress and anxiety symptoms characteristic of post-traumatic stress disorder. PTSD is a very serious, potentially life-threatening problem—a psychological reaction to an especially traumatic event. The symptoms commonly include flashbacks, nightmares, severe anxiety, hypervigilance, and powerful mood swings (including flashes of extreme anger, insecurity, and/or fear).

Have you noticed any of this behavior in your significant other? If so, it's your fault, not hers. She is just responding in a very normal way to the pain and hurt that you have caused. (By the way, she probably does not actually have PTSD; for a formal PTSD diagnosis, the symptoms must persist for at least six months, and what your partner is going through will probably abate, at least partially, within that timeframe.)

Regardless of how your mate has reacted since learning about your cheating, you have probably convinced yourself that your actions weren't that bad and you don't deserve all the grief she's heaping onto you. She, however, almost certainly feels otherwise. For proof, consider the results of a recent study on infidelity (Schneider, Weiss, and Samenow, 2012) in which betrayed women, after learning about their men's cheating, made statements like the following:

- "His cheating obliterated the trust in our relationship. I no longer believe a single thing he says."
- "We don't have sex often, and it irritates me that he puts more time into porn than in trying to be intimate with me."
- "I have been traumatized by his deception and betrayal."
- "I am over-the-top with snooping, spying, trying to control the behavior, and thinking that if I just find out everything then I could stop the cheating."
- "His cheating has caused complete erosion of my self-esteem, boundaries, and sense of self."
- "I feel unattractive and ugly, and I'm wondering what's wrong with me."
- "I can't sleep or concentrate."
- "I'm missing out on life's happiness."

While you're feeling resentful and impatient, wondering why your significant other won't just let this slide so you can both move on, she is likely suffering—deeply. And if you truly love her, you need to find a way to care about her pain and to support her instead of feeling rankled by her endless anger, demands, questions, withdrawal, and threats.

Do you remember the story of David, the king of Israel called "the man after God's own heart"? He also had many personal failings and challenges, including adultery. In fact, he had the husband of Bathsheba, his affair partner, killed to cover up his infidelity. David, though, did something that's astonishingly hard for most men to do: he humbled himself, took full responsibility for his sins, and begged God for forgiveness. There is the heart aspect again.

Finding patience and empathy for your wife's pain starts with feeling the depths of how you have betrayed her. This point isn't to shame you; in fact, it's just the opposite. It is an extraordinary act of faith and courage to admit your wrongs and put yourself in the shoes of the one you have hurt.

About "Gaslighting"

Gaslighting is a form of psychological abuse that involves the presentation of false information followed by dogged insistence that the information is true. Most people are familiar with this term thanks to *Gaslight*, the 1944 Oscar-winning film starring Ingrid Bergman and Charles Boyer. In the story, a husband tries to convince his new wife that she's imagining things, in particular the occasional dimming of their home's gaslights. This is part of the husband's plan to rob his wife of some very valuable jewelry. Over time, the wife, who trusts that her husband loves her and would never hurt her, starts to believe his lies and, in turn, to question her perception of reality and even her sanity. In the 21st century, the rather convoluted plot of *Gaslight* seems a bit silly. Nevertheless, the psychological concept of gaslighting—presenting false information and insisting that it's true, thereby causing the victim to question her or his perception of reality—is well accepted, particularly in connection with sexual infidelity.

Did you gaslight your partner to cover up your sexual adventures? If you think you didn't, you might want to think again. Consider the following lies:

- "I never said I'd be home by eight. I don't know why you'd think that."
- "She's just a coworker. When she calls here, it's because we have a project to finish. Why are you always so jealous?"
- "Why do you keep asking me if something is going on? You're completely paranoid. It's really annoying."
- "I told you I had to work late tonight. Obviously, you weren't listening."
- "I wasn't looking at her, I was looking over her shoulder to signal the waiter."
- "I told you at least three times that I might have to go out of town. When you don't listen like this, it feels like I don't matter to you. Why do you do this to me?"
- "I was working late at the office, closed my eyes for a minute, and fell asleep. I can't believe you're angry with me just because I forgot to call. How could I call when I was asleep?"
- "Who are you going to believe? Your nasty jealous sister or your loving husband?"
- "Honestly, I only work these late hours for us. For you, so we can have a better life. It's ridiculous that you think I'm cheating."
- "I would never do that. I don't even look at other women. You're just being crazy, and it really upsets me that you don't trust me."

Do any of these statements sound familiar? I'm guessing that at least a few of them do. Even if you didn't tell your spouse these exact lies, you almost certainly told similar whoppers. And when she worked up the courage to question your dishonesty, you flipped the script and insisted that your lies were true, that you weren't keeping secrets, and that she was either forgetful, delusional, or just making things up. You convinced her that *she* was the issue, and that her emotional reactions were the cause of, rather than the result of, the problems in your relationship. You made your spouse question her perception of reality.

At this point you might be thinking that you couldn't have pulled that off because your wife is way too smart to fall for that. But maybe that's not the case. One of the most disturbing facts about gaslighting is that even incredibly smart, emotionally well-adjusted people can fall for it. In part, this is because our natural tendency as human beings is to believe what we're told by the people we love. We will defend, excuse, and overlook our concerns about their behavior, especially when they seem sincere. In larger part, your spouse's vulnerability to gaslighting, no matter how smart or sane she usually is, is linked to the fact that gaslighting starts slowly and builds gradually over time. It's like placing a frog in a pot of warm water that is then set to boil. Because the temperature increases only gradually, the innocent frog never even realizes it's being cooked.

In the beginning, your lies probably seemed very plausible to your spouse. "I'm sorry I got home at midnight. I'm working on a very exciting project and I lost track of time." An excuse like that one sounds perfectly reasonable to a woman who both loves and trusts you, so it's easily accepted. She might even be excited about how interested you are in this new project at work. Of course, over time, as your cheating escalates, your deceptions also escalate. "I swear, I told you over breakfast that I was going away for the weekend. You were a little groggy, so maybe it didn't register. Or maybe you just forgot." Most women would toss that little doozy out with the garbage, but gaslighting victims become habituated over time to increasing levels of deceit, so eventually even the most outrageous lies seem plausible. Then, instead of questioning you, your betrayed and psychologically abused mate will question herself.

Certainly, you didn't mean to drive your partner crazy in this way. In fact, on some level it's likely that you were trying to protect her from the pain of learning about your cheating. Yet a lot of the problems wrought by infidelity are inadvertent and occurred because you didn't think about the potential consequences when you were tempted in the moment. Nevertheless, those consequences still occurred, whether you wanted them to or not, and you need to recognize and accept them if you hope to heal your relationship and make your way out of the doghouse.

Questions for Reflection

1. Does your wife seem more upset about your cheating than you think she should be? If so, in what ways?

2. What truths did your spouse uncover that you continued to lie about? (List at least five.) Did you tell those lies repeatedly and insist they were true?

3. Did you ever try to make your spouse believe that your relationship problems were all in her head? If so, how did you go about that? How do you feel about that behavior now?

CHAPTER FOUR

WHAT TO EXPECT FROM YOUR BETRAYED PARTNER

"Heaven has no rage like love to hatred turned, nor hell a fury like a woman scorned."
—William Congreve

When Trust is Shattered

As we discussed in the previous chapter, when cheating is discovered your spouse experiences it as a powerful form of emotional trauma. For her, it feels like being hit by a truck. In some ways the impact is also physical. She feels battered, bruised, and broken by what you've done. If she's invested in you, if she loves you and believes in you, and if she's committed to you, then she is devastated by your betrayal. There is just no avoiding that. And there is no avoiding her response. In fact, her rage, fear, pleading, tears, vindictiveness, and other forms of emotional instability—no matter how excessive this all seems to you—are perfectly normal and expected reactions in this set of circumstances.

It's not at all helpful to whine about her being crazy or worse, because in this case she's neither. Even if you really, really don't like the way she's acting (and you won't), and even if her behavior seems very, very dramatic to you (and it might), you need to accept that she is responding in an understandable and reasonably healthy way to the pain, loss, and hurt that you've caused her to feel.

Let's take a moment here to reinforce something stated earlier: Your spouse's deepest pain does not result from any particular extracurricular sex act that you engaged in; rather, her deepest pain comes from the shattering of relationship trust. The moment she found out you cheated, she lost the ability to fully trust you. You, the person closest to her—the one she thought would always have her back—hurt her by lying, keeping secrets, emotionally distancing yourself, and living a double life. As such, you have broken relationship trust. In her mind you were her best friend, her confidant, her lover, her financial partner, her co-parent, and her compatriot in life. And then you betrayed her by sneaking around and having sex with other women.

In your wife's eyes, you're like an athlete who secretly throws a game to win a bet. After an act that selfish, how can your teammates (or your wife, your kids, and anyone else you have betrayed) ever trust you again? Who could blame them for alternating between longing for the you they thought they knew, and despising the you who threw all their hard work and passion under the bus?

That's what your mate is feeling—only times a hundred! The most emotionally significant person in her life—the person around whom she has built her past, present, and future—has taken an emotional knife and stabbed her in the back with it, ripping her carefully constructed world apart with lies, manipulation, and a total lack of concern for her wellbeing.

Inside Her Emotions

In general, the degree of pain your partner experienced when she first learned about your infidelity hinged on the following five factors:

1. What you did
2. How long it went on
3. With whom you did it
4. How she found out
5. Her personal history of relationship safety

Let's examine each of these elements to help you understand what she might be thinking and feeling right now.

What You Did

Of the five factors listed above, the least important, by far, is what you did. Unless you've fallen in love with another woman, your wife doesn't much care whether you jerked off to porn, mutually masturbated via webcam, sexted with someone you met on Ashley Madison, got a hand-job in your car, or had intercourse with a woman you met at the grocery store. What she cares about is that you cheated.

As we've stated repeatedly, cheating is less about the actual sex act and more about the lies you told and the secrets you kept. It's not any specific sexual act that does the most damage, it's the betrayal of relationship trust. Whether she admits it or not, your significant other is more upset about the emotional chasm you've created than by the specifics of the sex you were having. Therefore, no matter what you did, you are likely to hear complaints like, "You never have time for me or the kids, but you somehow find time to sleep around. How can you treat me that way and still tell me that you love me?"

How Long It Went On

In terms of timeframe, a one-time sexual encounter while traveling on business is typically not as devastating, in the eyes of your mate, as a years-long affair. This is because, from her perspective, long-term affairs undercut everything that happened in your relationship while the affair was taking place. When your spouse learns that you've been sleeping with another woman for the last decade, she wonders, *All those times that he told me he loved me, and that he loved our kids and our life together, did he mean any of it? Or was it all just a lie? That time we went to the winery and we both had too much to drink and then we made love under an olive tree on the way back to the bed and breakfast—was he happy to be with me or was he fantasizing about her?* She might also be thinking about the time you missed your daughter's basketball game or some other important event, wondering, *Was he really at work, or was he having sex with her?*

With Whom You Did It

Your choice of affair partner matters in much the same way as the length of time. For instance, an affair with a woman that your spouse has never met and is unlikely to ever meet is nearly always less painful than an affair with a trusted neighbor, the nanny, her sister, or her best friend. If you've been sexual with someone she knows, that's double the trouble. And if that person happens to be someone she liked and/or trusted, the betrayal is doubled yet again. Further, if your affair partner is someone she's connected with in a spiritual sense, like singing in the choir together or sharing in a women's Bible study group, the pain is even worse, because now not only have you betrayed her, but her spiritual sister has, too. Each layer of connection increases her pain.

You should also keep in mind the fact that your wife will nearly always assume that there was an emotional component to your cheating—that you felt some sort of intimate bond with the other woman. This is true even if what you did was purely sexual in your viewpoint. Any evidence she finds that shows there really was an emotional connection just makes things worse. For example, if you've written warm, gushing letters to your affair partner, your spouse may be more upset about that than the actual sex. And if you gave your affair partner thoughtful gifts or took her on a romantic weekend getaway? Ouch! Especially if your significant other would have liked those gifts or trips for herself. In such cases, you might hear something like, "We always talked about going to New York in the springtime, but you took *her* instead! How could you do that?"

How She Found Out

Most people think that if they were in a supposedly monogamous relationship with a cheater, they would automatically know it. They mistakenly think that it would be almost impossible to miss the signs of sexual infidelity. However, this isn't necessarily the case. In fact, it's entirely possible, regardless of how many blatant clues you left, that your mate was unaware of your cheating. To a large extent this is because she didn't want to believe that you, her closest ally, could betray her, so she subconsciously chose to look the other way and engage in denial about what was happening. Even if she sensed that you were becoming emotionally distant, she probably convinced herself, perhaps with the help of your many "gentle suggestions" (i.e., manipulations), that there was some other cause: you were preoccupied with work, you were worried about finances, or whatever.

It sometimes seems as if the betrayed wife is always the last to know about her man's extracurricular sexual activities. And that makes a lot of sense. After all, a guy who cheats is usually going to focus a lot more on hiding things from his spouse than from the rest of the world. Moreover, in a general way we are inclined to not notice the eccentric, unusual, or erratic behavior of others, especially the people we are close to. And when we do notice, we often create excuses for what the other person is doing. This is particularly true in family settings, where spouses (and kids) *need to believe* that their significant other (or their parent) is trustworthy and dependable and consistently doing the right thing.

Is it any wonder that betrayed partners are often the last to know? Even women who suspect infidelity may unconsciously opt for ignorance, hoping that their suspicions aren't true. Often, they choose to disregard the problem for as long as they can—usually for emotional reasons (love, fear of being alone), practical reasons (kids, finances), or to avoid pain.

Unfortunately, the unexpected nature of the revelation is only part of your partner's pain. The method in which the information is delivered can be equally, if not more, disturbing. For instance, there's a huge difference between her learning about your infidelity when you remorsefully and voluntarily confess the truth versus the following:

- Walking in on you with your pants down—literally
- Getting an anonymous phone call
- Hearing about it from a group of friends who assumed she already knew (because everyone else certainly did)
- Discovering your stash of porn, your sexting, and your use of hookup apps when she borrows your phone or laptop
- Being called by the police because you're in jail, snared in a prostitution sting
- Being told by her physician that she has a sexually transmitted disease

There's finding out about your cheating, and there's *finding out* about your cheating.

Regardless of how your significant other learns about your infidelity, discovery shock is an almost universal reaction. In part, this stems from the fact that while you've known about your cheating from the start (and you may actually be feeling a sense of relief now that your behavior is out in the open), your loved one has just been blindsided by this information. She isn't just learning about it, she's getting emotionally body-slammed by it. Even partners who had a previous sense that something was amiss with the relationship will experience the trauma of discovery when their worst fears are confirmed.

For a comparison, think about a lingering illness. For a few months you feel unwell. You're tired a lot, and you have a pesky cough that just won't go away. Eventually you decide to go to the doctor, hoping for some antibiotics that will clear things up. Instead, after a careful examination, you are hit with the news that you have a life-threatening illness. Even if you suspected deep down that you might have a serious problem, you still feel blindsided when you learn about it.

That is precisely what your wife feels like when she learns about your cheating.

Her Personal History of Relationship Safety

The degree and duration of your significant other's reaction to infidelity may be related as much to her early life history as to your betrayal. If she was abused, neglected, or otherwise traumatized in the past (by parents, siblings, teachers, or old boyfriends), her sense of relationship safety may already be compromised, which causes her to more deeply react to the present situation. Thus, she may be reacting to much more than your sexual betrayal. She might also be reacting, in delayed fashion, to her father's alcoholism and his abandonment of her mother, the fact that she and her sister were molested by a family friend, the fact that her first boyfriend dumped her without warning and started dating her rival, and a whole lot of other stuff that you may not even know about. Basically, if your mate has ever been deceived, abandoned, abused, neglected, or otherwise mistreated by a beloved and/or trusted person, she may have some deep emotional wounds as a result—wounds that will never really go away. Your present-day cheating has probably reopened those wounds and poured salt in them. If so, you may be paying for crimes you didn't commit.

It's possible you're now thinking, *That's unfair!* And maybe it is. But you need to get over it, because it's a fact of life that you're going to have to accept and work with if you want to save your relationship. Your partner's history of trauma is what it is. If she was betrayed, neglected, or otherwise abused, then that trauma—no matter when it occurred—will almost certainly resurface because of your cheating. This is your mate's emotional reality, and it's your reality as well. If you could change this aspect of who she is, we would gladly tell you how. But you cannot, so our suggestion is that you not try. You can't control it, and you can't fix it. All you can do is accept it and learn to work with it.

If anything, your mate's personal history of prior relationship trauma is your invitation to extra measures of compassion. You may have been aware of the pain she experienced from her alcoholic father and heard her insistence that she would never marry an alcoholic. And she didn't. She married a cheater, which isn't an improvement. Your opportunity is to hold her heart even more gently as she reels from the pain of your infidelity.

Are you still surprised that your wife has responded with fear, anger, rage, and a variety of other strong emotions after learning about your cheating? We hope not. In fact, we hope that by now you're beginning to see that in your wife's eyes your cheating has many layers, and those layers permeate every aspect of her existence. For her, it's not just the sex, it's everything.

The Emotional Roller Coaster

In the immediate aftermath of discovery, your significant other's emotions were understandably out of control. And you're probably okay with that because you expected it to some extent. Unfortunately for you, her reactivity is unlikely to dissipate any time soon. In fact, you're going to have to deal with the emotional roller coaster she's riding until you've re-earned her trust. And that healing process can take many long months.

For your wife there is no such thing as immediate forgiveness when it comes to relationship betrayal. Even worse, she will never forget. In her mind, there is *before the infidelity* and *after the infidelity*. The fact that you betrayed her trust is not something she will easily move past. So, for the time being you should expect her to engage in or display some (or all) of the following perfectly normal symptoms of deep emotional betrayal:

- **Detective work.** Because your spouse no longer trusts you, she will probably seek out the truth by doing detective work. Searching for evidence of infidelity, she might check your phone bills, your browser history, your e-mails, your text messages, the contents of your wallet, your credit card receipts and bills, your phone apps, and more. She might hire an actual private detective to help with this. She might surreptitiously install tracking software on your phone and other digital devices. And this hypervigilant behavior is likely to occur even if you're now being completely open and honest about your whereabouts and actions.
- **Mood swings.** Your mate may be sad one minute, filled with rage the next, and then desperately affectionate, loving, and even sexual the next. And her moods might swing from one extreme to the other with little or no warning. The most innocuous triggers are likely to set her off. For instance, you could happily be watching a movie on TV and one of the actresses may look like your affair partner (or how your significant other suspects your affair partner looked), and off she goes—tearful and raging. Then, five minutes later, she may be apologetic and remorseful.
- **Shame and loss of self-esteem.** For many of us, our self-esteem is tied (at least in part) to having a successful relationship and family life. In other words, your wife may have worked very hard to create the best possible "us." If so, her self-esteem will have understandably taken a huge hit because of your infidelity. She might suddenly feel unattractive and unlovable, no matter the reality or how

much you tell her otherwise. In response, she might overcompensate by trying to lose weight, dressing provocatively, or trying to be hypersexual with you, thinking that if she can somehow "get it right" you will stop fooling around on her. Or she may withdraw completely.

- **Global mistrust.** By cheating, you have violated your mate's trust in you and your relationship. This trust must be re-earned, and that takes both time and effort. For now, you need to accept that she will question every little thing you do and say. If you arrive home five minutes late, turn off your computer too quickly, or play with your iPhone without telling her what app you're using, her mistrust may be triggered. She will also doubt you in other areas of life: finances, childcare, or even dinner reservations. Her reasoning is that if you lied to her about something as important as sex, you're capable of lying to her about absolutely anything.
- **Control.** Because her relationship feels out of control and she no longer trusts anything you say or do, your spouse may try to micromanage things like family finances, childcare, your free time, and chores. You might not have much say about the day-to-day rhythm and decision making of your relationship. Even worse, she will probably resent you for "forcing her" into all this extra work.
- **Raging and attacking.** If you think that going on the attack is the sole province of men, think again. To paraphrase the quote that opened this chapter: Hell hath no fury like a woman scorned. Your partner may at times behave like a feral cat backed into a corner, hissing and snarling and lashing out. She will attack you verbally, call you names, devalue the good things you do, and basically hit below the belt in any way she can. She might also hire a lawyer, tell the kids what you've done, recklessly spend money to punish you, have an affair of her own to get

even, toss your clothes onto the front lawn, or hammer your car with a nine iron.
- **Obsessive questioning.** It may seem as though your wife is obsessed with your cheating, as if there's no subject on the planet that interests her more than your betrayal. She wants to know what happened, where, with whom, how many times, and all sorts of other minute details. Her obsession may cause her to experience sleeplessness, nightmares, difficulty concentrating, or an inability to focus on day-to-day events. And no matter how much information you give, she will ask for more. Then, when you stop providing information, even if it's because there is no more to give, she'll accuse you of holding back.
- **Avoidance.** This is the opposite of obsessive questioning, but it's equally likely. Basically, your spouse may work to avoid thinking or talking about your betrayal. She may pretend that the cheating never happened. She might even avoid talking and interacting with you altogether, except for the most superficial communication. Even more perplexing is that she might flip-flop between obsessive questioning and avoidance. One minute she'll want to know everything, and the next she'll want to bury her head in the sand.
- **Escapist (including addictive) behavior.** Your significant other may be so distressed by your cheating and the inherent breach of relationship trust that she needs to temporarily escape her feelings. Drinking, drugging, binge eating, compulsive spending, compulsive gambling, compulsive use of social media, compulsive exercise, and compulsive sexual activity are all common responses.

None of these perfectly natural responses are fun for you to deal with, of course. In fact, the emotional roller coaster that you and your betrayed partner are riding is very likely to aggravate you at least occasionally, no matter how understanding you are about the fact that you are the cause of this wild and unpleasant ride. When you do get angry, you'll need to make a choice. You can react to her emotions and make things worse, or you can swallow your pride, your ego, and your desire to be right, and allow her to feel whatever it is that she needs to feel. We rather strongly suggest the latter.

Understanding Broken Trust from a Neutral Perspective

To better understand what your spouse is feeling, consider the following analogy. You are a small-business owner and you hire a down-on-his-luck friend to help you in the office. He has the necessary skills, more or less, and you want to help him because you like him. One day you come into work early and catch him with his hand in the safe, and you've recently noticed that the petty cash accounting has been off. Because this person is a friend, you verbally rip into him, but you don't fire him. You put him on probation but keep him on the payroll. And he is incredibly grateful. Things are great for the next year or so. Then one night you're staying late at work, and you notice him in the office alone with the door of the safe pulled open. What is your immediate reaction? If you're like most people, you immediately flash back to the day you caught him stealing. And this will happen even if he's currently doing nothing wrong.

Well, your relationship is quite similar. If your spouse sees you doing anything that even remotely reminds her of when you cheated, her mistrust will be triggered again—even if you're not doing anything wrong at that moment. And that's a perfectly natural reaction for her to have.

Pills You Don't Have to Swallow

It is okay (even expected) that your significant other will be incredibly angry with you and that she will (in your eyes) consistently overreact to any perceived slight. It's wise for you to accept these reactions within reason. If, however, she crosses the line, you can try to set some boundaries, perhaps with the assistance of an experienced couple's therapist.

Unacceptable reactions from your mate include the following:

- Hitting or any other form of physical violence, including hitting walls or breaking furniture
- Turning your kids or other family members against you
- Telling your boss, your neighbors, the press, or other important people what you've done, especially in a vindictive way rather than as a means of getting support
- Devaluing your humanity by saying things like, "You don't deserve to live"
- Going to the other woman to give her a piece of her mind

If your partner is behaving in ways that cause you to fear for your physical and/or emotional wellbeing or the wellbeing of those around you, especially your children, you don't have to sit back and take it. You shouldn't, however, respond in kind. Instead, you should politely explain that her actions have crossed the line and that you need to set up some fair fighting boundaries. (Resolving conflicts in healthy, nondestructive ways is discussed in detail in chapter nine.)

What It Means to Be in the Doghouse

Once they've been found out, many men who've cheated think that a simple puppy dog apology and maybe a nice necklace or a romantic vacation should remedy the situation. They seem to think that the words *I'm sorry* should automatically initiate immediate and total forgiveness—that if they show even a semblance of remorse (no matter how insincere), the relationship should magically revert to how it was before they cheated. In fact, if you're like most of the men who are confronted with their cheating behavior, you instinctively attempted the guy's seven-step version of an apology, which typically goes as follows:

1. "Yes, I did it."
2. "I'm sorry."
3. "I never meant to hurt you."
4. "I won't do it again."
5. "What can I do to make it right?"
6. "I hope you will forgive me."
7. "What's for lunch?"

If you tried this tactic, we're guessing that it didn't go too well. In fact, you're probably reading this book because your spouse didn't think your apology was enough to re-earn her trust. Instead of accepting your expression of regret and forgiving you, she has banished you to the doghouse, and now you're going to have to jump through a whole lot of hoops before she lets you out.

By this point, we hope you understand how your partner is experiencing this blow to your relationship. If not, we suggest that you go back to the beginning of the book and read these first four chapters again. If, however, you think you might be ready to begin the healing process, read on, because the remainder of this book is dedicated to helping you and your spouse move forward toward rebuilding your lives and your relationship.

Questions for Reflection

1. Do you think that your cheating deserves the kind of reaction you are getting from your spouse? Why or why not?

2. In what ways has your cheating affected how your spouse sees you and your relationship? (Consider what you did, how long it went on, with whom you did it, how she found out, and her history of relationship trauma.)

3. Does your spouse seem to be riding an emotional roller coaster? If so, can you understand why? And if you do have a sense of why, what can you do to accept this as a normal and even healthy response on her part?

4. Read Psalm 51 and perhaps even copy or type it into your journal. Write another paragraph to God about increasing your ownership of your infidelity and your empathy for your wife's pain.

CHAPTER FIVE

TO STAY OR GO?

> "Two roads diverged in a wood, and I—
> I took the one less traveled by,
> And that has made all the difference."
> —Robert Frost, *The Road Not Taken*

It's Not Necessarily Based on What You Think You Want

If you're like most guys who get caught cheating, you probably experienced one or perhaps a combination of the three reactions listed below:

1. **Clarity, version one.** Discovery of your cheating caused you to realize how much you truly value your spouse and how much you want to heal your relationship. When you were finally confronted about your infidelity and asked to decide—*her or me?*—you knew immediately, deep in your soul, that you wanted to stay with your long-term mate no matter the cost. Before that moment you may have bounced easily from your wife to other women and then back to your wife. But suddenly, with your relationship on

the line, you realized that you'd been risking the one thing in your life that matters the most.
2. **Clarity, version two.** Revelation of your infidelity propelled you into facing the reality that your marriage was in deep trouble even before you cheated. Your relationship had struggled painfully for a long time in ways that one or both of you ignored or glossed over. The ship was sinking already, and your infidelity was the huge wave that swamped it completely. You wondered if you married the wrong person, if the relationship could or should be saved. At the very least, the emotional bond between you and your wife had disintegrated to the point where it was almost nonexistent. And now you understand that the best way to handle this collapse is directly, by either attempting to address the issues or walking away.
3. **Indecision.** Your spouse's discovery of your infidelity forced you to examine both your primary relationship and your cheating, and you realized that you want to continue with both. You understood that your mate provides stability and a home life, whereas your infidelity provides excitement and escape from what feels like an otherwise unexciting existence. One minute you love your spouse and your relationship with her seems like the most important thing in the world, but just a little while later you can't bear the thought of life without cheating, at least just a little. You are a "double-minded" man (Jas. 1:8).

Our rather strong guess, based solely on the fact that you're still reading this book, is that you fall into either the first or the third category.

If you fall into the first category, good for you, because it will be a lot easier to walk away from your past behavior and focus on what's important in the future.

If you fall into the second category, it's possible that you got into your marriage quickly or for the wrong reasons. Maybe you were young and inexperienced and didn't know any better. Maybe you felt pressured by your or her family for whatever reason (e.g., religion or pregnancy). If so, now is your chance to step back and reassess yourself as well as your relationship. Guilt, shame, fear of being alone, fear of financial insecurity, and fear of what other people will think of you aren't good foundations for rebuilding a marriage.

If you're in category three, struggling to know what you really want, you needn't despair, because this chapter will help you identify some next right steps for you and those around you.

> Note: This chapter is worth reading even if you're already certain that you want to stay in or walk away from your primary relationship, because it will help deepen your understanding of your reasons.

Making the decision about staying with your mate and working on your marriage versus leaving the relationship can be confusing, especially if you are facing (and feeling overwhelmed by) your wife's heated emotions. If you've had an emotionally charged long-term affair and that woman and her feelings also enter the fray, the situation gets even tougher. In such cases, you might find that you have two women demanding a decision, and they will probably want your answer *right this instant.* In addition, you almost certainly realize that any decision you make is going to affect the rest of your life, not to mention the lives of your kids, your spouse, your affair partner(s), friends, family, and others.

Having Your Cake and Eating It Too

If you've been having a long-term affair, you may find yourself thinking that you love both women equally. You just can't imagine your life without either one of them in it. You're tempted to smooth things over in the short term, and then (deceitfully, of course) continue with both your marriage and your affair. If so, be warned: Even though having your cake and eating it, too, might seem like a great idea to you, it will almost certainly blow up in your face. When your wife discovers your continuing infidelity (after your promises and assurances that you've stopped) your marriage is almost guaranteed to be over. Equally important, this selfish, sinful, and cowardly plan prohibits you from being the man of integrity God calls you to be.

If You Stay

Assuming you opt to reinvest in your marriage, you need to understand that no matter how hard you work to restore it, things will never go back to the way they were before you cheated. After all, you've betrayed your wife on the deepest level, and she will never forget that fact. At the very least, she will never again implicitly trust you the way she once did. As Rob's mother used to say, you can't un-bake a cake. The damage is done, and your relationship cannot ever return to what it once was. (The good news is that marriages that have weathered these storms and made the effort to rebuild are usually better than before. Both partners have been to the brink of destruction, have rebuilt from the ground up, and are grateful to be on the other side.)

Even worse, repairing a broken relationship is a lengthy and often unpleasant process. For starters, you'll almost certainly have to come clean about *all* of your cheating, not just the parts your significant other already knows about. You'll have to become totally honest about everything else, too, even when the truth hurts and angers her. You'll have to sit quietly while she rages at you for no apparent reason. You'll have to relinquish all sorts of privacy. You'll have to put up with her questioning your every move and even the thoughts you might be having.

Getting out of the doghouse isn't a leisurely stroll in the park. Despite your desire to restore your marriage, at times it will seem that ending it would be easier and cleaner for you both. But if you walk away from the woman you still love, what have you gained? More likely, both of you will lose. Don't quit!

For an analogy, let's turn to the sports world. In 2004, Shaun Livingston was a tall, lanky, eighteen-year-old point guard generally regarded as a can't-miss NBA prospect. Based on that, he skipped college, entered the NBA draft, and was selected fourth overall by the Los Angeles Clippers. In 2007, just as he was approaching NBA superstardom, he shredded the inner workings of his left knee. Basically, the only thing connecting his thigh to his calf was skin, and even though there had been many advances in modern orthopedics, nearly everyone assumed that his basketball career was over. There just wasn't any way he was ever going to regain the quickness and explosiveness that made him a star.

Livingston could have taken the easy way out, deciding that his career was over, and nobody would have blamed him. After all, he'd earned millions already. He was also personable and intelligent enough to launch a second career as a commentator, coach, or front office executive.

But Livingston made another choice: He spent almost two years rehabilitating his knee and another five years bouncing from team to team (ten in all) trying to reestablish himself. Finally, in the summer of 2014, after a solid season playing mostly as a backup for a woeful Brooklyn Nets team, he signed a long-term deal with the Golden State Warriors, where he became one of the league's most valuable role players. He also helped Golden State to its first NBA title in forty years.

Livingston today is certainly not the basketball player that he once was. His game is vastly different and relies more on brains and skill than sheer athleticism. But his on-court contributions are as valuable as ever, and he's got a championship ring to prove it—all because he chose the unpleasantly rocky path of healing and decided to save his seemingly demolished playing career no matter what.

For Livingston, the decision to rehab his knee and suffer all sorts of indignities—pay cuts, trades (three times), being released (four times), ten-day contracts (twice), and a demeaning stint in the NBA's Developmental League—couldn't have been easy. He surely must have experienced a great deal of ambivalence, frustration, shame, and uncertainty along the way. But he always confronted the decision-making process intelligently, weighing the pros and cons and ultimately concluding that his love of playing the game outweighed his dislike and fear of injuries, rejection, and career and financial instability.

The process of deciding whether to stay in and repair a damaged relationship is, in many ways, like Shaun Livingston's basketball journey. When you're thinking about whether to save your relationship or move on to something else, even if you find that you're tortured with mood swings and indecisiveness, you should absolutely not make a hasty choice. Take time to weigh the pros and cons and fully consider all aspects of your decision.

Healing after infidelity requires more fortitude than you may have considered. Jesus told his followers to consider the cost of being a disciple and provided two practical examples. The first was someone who wants to build a tower, and the second was a king who was about to go into battle. Both were advised to count the cost of their undertakings (Luke 14:28-33). In similar fashion, be prepared to pay the price of restoration. This process grows you as a person—your character, your patience, your humility, your selflessness—and it grows your relationship with God.

To Stay or Go: Fourteen Questions to Ask Yourself

Before we look at some practical questions to guide your decision-making, it's important to wrestle first with a more fundamental one: *What exactly is the purpose of marriage, anyway?* The media and our culture have an immediate answer: my happiness, of course! Remember, you were attempting to pursue happiness by your cheating, right? And it landed you (deservedly) in the doghouse.

A faith perspective offers an alternative premise: maybe marriage is more of a chance to mature you and make you more like Christ than it is to make you happy in the usual sense. Sure, a healthy relationship is fun, rewarding, and fulfilling. (Thank you, God.) But a covenant relationship is also difficult, challenging, boring, and downright painful, at times, even if infidelity never darkens the relationship doors.

Be sure that your life's focus is on developing a deeper daily relationship with the Divine more than on a relationship with a person, including your spouse. When that higher priority guides your thinking and behavior, you'll be more clear about the path ahead.

Of course, there is no cut-and-dried formula for deciding if your committed relationship has enough positive aspects to make the difficult work of healing worthwhile. Nevertheless, by honestly answering the questions below you'll likely gain some degree of clarity, especially if your answers are supplemented with honest, empathetic, and impartial feedback from a therapist, a trusted friend, a spiritual advisor, and/or a supportive family member.

1. **Do you share core values and beliefs?** To make a relationship work over the long haul you need at least some common ground regarding things like values, religion, finances, education, politics, and raising kids. If you have this in your relationship, then you have a solid foundation upon which you can rebuild. Conversely, your relationship's potential is significantly diminished if one of you feels forced into a certain belief system or way of living and accepts it only to make the other person happy

or to avoid rejection and abandonment. Obviously, you and your mate aren't going to agree on everything, including some key issues. But if you don't have basic respect for your partner's viewpoint regarding a core value, that's a significant problem.
2. **Do you have kids?** Children aren't the only reason to stay in a relationship, but they're a darn good one. After all, no matter how much you struggle with your spouse, your love for your children continues, and you'll always keep their welfare in mind. You need to consider the ways in which they'll be affected if you and your spouse separate. You should also keep in mind that your ex will probably get at least half-time custody if you split up, so you won't see your kids nearly as often, which is distressing for everybody. (If the children are hers from a previous relationship, you might not see them at all.) In short, breaking up a family is a significantly more profound decision than splitting up a couple, because the lives and futures of several people, some of whom may be too young to fend for themselves, are at stake.
3. **Do you trust her?** Trust is a key element in a healthy relationship. If two people trust each other, if they know they have each other's backs no matter what, that's a solid relationship foundation. Of course, you've almost certainly decimated your partner's trust in you by cheating on her, and it will take a long time and a lot of concerted effort to earn back that trust. The question here, really, is whether you still trust her to be there for you. If you do, that's worth a lot; in fact, it's downright amazing considering what you've done. How many people in this world would you trust with your home, your finances, your kids, your feelings, and everything else that's important in your life?
4. **Do you enjoy spending time with her?** If you have come to genuinely dislike (or no longer appreciate) your spouse as a person, or you have lost respect for her for

whatever reason (not relating to her reaction to your infidelity), that's an obvious red flag. After all, one of the primary benefits of being in a long-term romantic partnership is that it's fun and enjoyable. If you find that you dread spending time with your wife, if being with her feels like a chore, then you may lack a solid relationship support beam. That reality doesn't necessarily mean you should leave, but it's a hard truth that will take extra effort to overcome.

5. **Do you and your spouse usually find a way to resolve disagreements?** In any intimate relationship, conflict is inevitable. It's also useful because it helps us to define our boundaries and desires. In healthy relationships, arguments and disagreements are growth opportunities—chances to learn patience, empathy, and new ways of thinking and relating. However, when a relationship isn't so healthy, even the smallest issue can become a smoldering resentment (usually tied to other, much deeper and more enduring concerns). Even when you and your spouse are unable to agree, if you can at least amicably disagree most of the time, then you probably have something worth saving.

6. **Are you free to be your own man?** Yes, good relationships are built on commonality, but too much closeness and agreement can feel smothering and enmeshed (to both of you). If you feel uncomfortable with or discouraged from having your own interests, friends, and activities (not including your cheating), then you may be in an excessively entangled, fear-based relationship, and that's far from ideal. The best relationships involve separate people with separate identities, with each person free to think and act as he or she sees fit (within certain mutually agreed-upon limits).

7. **Is there basic equality in the relationship?** If you and your partner each bring something special and meaningful

to the relationship, then it's much easier to respect each other's opinions, interests, beliefs, and contributions. If, however, the relationship is drastically unequal, with one person running the show at all times, you'll probably continue to struggle. In a healthy relationship, each person values and respects the other exactly as he or she truly is. This isn't to say there can't be different capabilities and roles in certain areas. For instance, one of you likely makes more money or has a more easily recognized status like a high-powered position (instead of the vastly harder work of staying home with young kids). There's nothing wrong with this arrangement, as long as neither of you feels used, put-upon, exploited, or unappreciated, and the lines of communication are open regarding growth and change.

8. **Does she support you emotionally?** If you think that your mate isn't there for you when the going gets tough or that she expresses constant disagreement, dismissal, negativity, criticism, control, or indifference toward your thoughts, beliefs, goals, desires, or activities (aside from your sexual infidelity), that's not a great indicator of long-term relationship wellbeing. If, however, she works to help you succeed and leaves you feeling as if you consistently have someone in your corner cheering for you, then your relationship is much more likely to survive.

9. **Does your relationship roll with the punches?** It's important for both you and your wife to understand that a relationship isn't stagnant. If growth occurs or is sought, and both parties accept and even cheer that process, then there is a great foundation on which to rebuild.
Conversely, the more resistance there is to change, the tougher it will be to heal your relationship, because a major part of the healing process involves making changes.

10. **Do you play well together?** If you and your mate have at least a few common interests—hobbies and activities that you can enjoy together—that's a positive relationship

indicator, especially if those interests are an important area of life for one or both of you. This means that if you and your mate find each other's activities, recreational pursuits, and anecdotes fun and entertaining (or at least not too boring), then the two of you probably enjoy being together. This doesn't mean that you must love all her interests, nor she yours. If her passion for bird watching puts you to sleep, so be it, as long as the two of you have at least a few interests that you both enjoy.

11. **Are your relationship expectations realistic?** No person or relationship is perfect. If either you or your spouse consistently expects the other to look and act in a certain way, then disappointment is inevitable. In a healthy relationship, both partners must accept and respect each other, warts and all. No person can consistently live up to another person's fantasy of perfection, and expecting someone to do so is a recipe for disappointment, resentment, pain, and failure.

12. **Do you still enjoy sex with her?** You're probably well past the puppy-love stage when you first started having sex, and you don't feel the same type of electric shock with your wife that you get when you're with a hot new woman. The question here isn't about having the crazy-wild "I have to have you now!" feeling every time you look at your spouse. It's about whether you feel a continuing spark of sexual attraction to her and if you enjoy the physical intimacy that you still have with her (or that you *were* having until she found out about your cheating). Yes, this question is intentionally toward the bottom of the list. Don't compare your sexual desire and satisfaction with your spouse with your sextracurricular activities—that's unfair and unrealistic.

13. **Have you done this before?** Do you have a history of ending relationships because of your cheating? If so, no matter how you feel about your significant other, it's

probably time to take a long hard look at your thoughts and behaviors regarding long-term commitment. If the common denominator in your failed relationships is you, the happiness that you seek will never be found by simply moving on to someone new. Our strong encouragement is to stick with your current relationship while you make changes within yourself. If you do, you may find that you end up with something truly special.

14. **Are you both invested in saving the relationship?** It takes two to tango. If you want to restore your relationship but your mate seems determined to end it, there's little you can do about that stalemate. If your desire to save your relationship is one-sided, then there really is no longer a relationship to save. In such cases, the best that you can do is accept this fact, grieve, treat your wife with kindness and respect during the parting, and learn from your mistakes. (Please note that many women say they are done in the heat of the moment but don't really mean it. If you think this might the case with your spouse, then don't give up. But if she really does seem finished, you may need to just back away and move on.)

Again, there are no set rules for determining when a relationship is or isn't worth saving. Nor is this book written to convince you to either stay or move on—with the caveat of Marnie's sincere belief in the premise about marriage that opens this section, which is biased toward staying and working for restoration. Sadly, though, some relationships are plagued with other intractable problems that have nothing to do with your infidelity, which is a situation beyond the scope of this book. Ultimately, you must decide this matter for yourself. If, however, you find that you've answered yes to more than a few of the above questions, then you've probably got something that is easily worth the effort.

We'd also like to reiterate that it's wise to share your responses to the above questions above with other people: a therapist, a spiritual advisor, trusted friends, or supportive family members. These are people who know you and your relationship well, and, as impartial observers, they can see and point out the things that you may be missing or ignoring. In all likelihood, you'll find their input invaluable, even if you don't always like what they say in the moment.

Do You Need More Time?

It's entirely possible that you still haven't made a definite decision about staying or going, even with the clarity you got from the questions above. A part of you may still want to continue with both your primary relationship and your cheating. You may even find yourself changing your mind every five or ten minutes about which seems more important.

If you keep waffling between your marriage and your infidelity, you can try to postpone your decision for six weeks or so, giving yourself (and the women in your life) time to calm down and think more clearly. This is best done with guidance from a therapist.

If you choose to play for time in this way, *do not tell your mate that you are unsure you want to stay with her*. If you do that, she is likely to render your assessment process moot by deciding that she's not willing to wait. If she tells you, "It's me or her, and you need to decide *right now*," we suggest you respond with something like, "I'm not planning to leave you. But please give me some time to get my head cleared, even though I don't deserve it after what I've done." You might even want to ask for some time apart, assuring her that you don't want this to be long-term. She will probably not like that idea (unless it's hers rather than yours), but you are unlikely to gain the clarity you need while you're still residing in an angry household.

If you and your spouse decide to take some time apart, this doesn't mean that it's time to move in with your affair partner! You need to step away from her, too. As a rule, we suggest that rather than moving into a hotel room or an apartment of your own, where you'll probably feel bored, lonely, and tempted to cheat, you move in with your parents, a sibling, or a close friend. You'll get much needed emotional support there, and cheating will be much less of an option.

One difficulty that you may encounter is that your affair partner could be just as unhappy as your spouse about your requested time-out. If so, your approach with her should be the same as with your wife. Ask for time apart so you can clear your head and make a good decision. Whatever you do, don't lie to your affair partner about time you'll be spending with your wife. And don't lie about anything else, either. In other words, don't tell your affair partner that you're planning to leave your wife so you can be with her, unless you have unequivocally made up your mind to do so (and have considered this decision for a few days or weeks to be certain).

Lastly, it's very important for you to understand and accept that taking time to think things through is exactly that—a temporary time-out with the goal of wise reflection. It's *not* any of the following:

- Continuing to see, call, text, or email your affair partner
- Sneaking off for a booty call in a weak and lonely moment
- Texting or sexting with other women
- Continuing to lie and keep secrets from your spouse
- Bouncing from one woman to the other and then back again to see which one you like best
- Checking hookup apps "just to see who's out there"
- Going online for pornography or webcam sex
- Flirting with women at work
- Going out for drinks with your buddies and hitting on the waitress

No More Cheating!

Regardless of your current indecision, if you ask for time to sort things out, then you absolutely must stop cheating. Completely and totally. Right now. You just flat out cannot tell your wife that you are putting your relationship with her on temporary hold so you can clear your head, and then continue to engage in infidelity. That's something she will never forgive. *Never.* (Unless she's a true saint or gets a direct vision from God, which isn't something you should count on.)

Decision Time

Regardless of whether your infidelity was casual or emotionally connected, there are three primary considerations about your marriage that are worth reflection: the past, the present, and the future. If you find yourself comparing one relationship to another, as you're likely to do with an emotionally connected affair, you need to understand that this isn't an apples-to-apples comparison. It's more like apples-to-cookies. Your fourteen-year marriage with two kids isn't comparable to your relationship with a hot twenty-five-year-old (or another 40-year-old) who thinks everything you do is magical. These are just entirely different things.

With your wife you have a history, home, family, friends, intermingled finances, standing in the community and church, and all sorts of roles and responsibilities. With your affair partner you have the excitement of illicit sex but little of the rest, even if you believe you have something deeper. You've likely never had to mow her lawn, pay her bills, take out her garbage, pick up groceries on your way home after a long day at work, live with her bad moods, or take care of her when she's ill. And even if you have done some or all of those things, it's not the same as being in a covenant marriage. By definition, an affair is an *other*—and from a faith perspective, it is categorically and unequivocally outside the bounds of God's plan for sex and relationships. It's forbidden fruit, which by Satan's design always tastes sweeter.

Discipline yourself to lean into a bias toward your marriage as a starting point. Again, that's the purpose of a covenant relationship: It's a *holy, spiritual covenant*, which means it's a sacred pledge that is not quickly dismissed.

Looking at Your Past

As you work on making your decision, start by thinking about your history with your spouse. And make sure you don't rewrite it just because she's incredibly angry and unpleasant right now. After all, you're the one who cheated, and that's why she's so upset. Put aside your current marital distress and look at life with your wife *before* you sullied the relationship and earned your trip to the doghouse. Ask yourself the following:

- What qualities attracted me to her in the first place (beyond her physical appearance)?
- What qualities made me fall in love with her? Does she still possess those qualities? Are those qualities that I still value?
- If my relationship with her ended today, what would I miss the most?

By the way, we strongly suggest that you *not* ask yourself these questions about your long-term affair partner, though you will be automatically tempted to go there. Indulging in that reflection will only cause you to miss her more and cloud your thinking.

Looking at Your Present

When you're analyzing the present, it's again important that you push aside your mate's justifiable anger so you can look at the situation objectively. Ask yourself the following about your spouse:

- Do I love her?
- Do I like her and enjoy spending time with her?
- Do I care about the life that we have built together: our home, our friends, our children, and our shared interests?
- Am I willing to do the work of healing, no matter how unpleasant that may at times become?

Looking at Your Future

Now think about the future. Ask yourself the following:

- What do I want my life to look like five years from now?
- What do I want my life to look like twenty years from now? Who, if anyone, do I want to be with?
- How will my children (and other family members) be affected if I stay in my primary relationship? If I end my marriage and move on with my affair partner? If I choose divorce and move on as a single man (for a while, at least)?
- Can my primary relationship heal and perhaps become stronger than ever if I re-earn my wife's trust? And if I don't, will I ever behave in a trustworthy way in future relationships? If I go with my affair partner instead of my wife, will I end up cheating on her, too?

Breaking the News

Whatever decision you make, you need to tell the women involved. And while you shouldn't rush the decision-making process, you shouldn't delay informing them once you have considered the facts and reached a firm decision. In other words, don't string your spouse or an affair partner along just because you're dreading the pain of giving her some bad news. And regardless of your decision, remember that your goal is to move forward with integrity, which means no longer lying to your spouse or anyone else about your romantic intentions.

If you decide to stay with your wife and your infidelity was of the casual variety, where you didn't feel much (if any) emotional connection to your cheating partners, it should be fairly easy to break things off with them. You can simply delete their contact information from your phone and computer, unfriend them on social media, delete your hookup apps and profiles, delete any texts and/or photos related to your cheating, and move forward. Sure, a past sex partner might try to contact you occasionally for a quickie, but all you have to do is say, "No thank you," and then block her number so she can't call again. You don't even have to worry about upsetting her, because you (hopefully) didn't lead her on in a way that would cause her to feel overly attached.

If you decide to stay with your significant other even though you've been in a long-term affair with a woman that you care about, things are much more difficult. Likely you will balk at the idea of simply breaking things off, especially if you've grown heavily entangled in her life. After all, this is a person you care about, who cares about you in return, and ending the relationship is going to hurt her. A lot. Despite the pain involved for both of you, do not skimp on this step! As recovery language puts it, be fearless from the very start. When you've made your decision, inform your affair partner—*by phone, email, or letter, not in person.* Then follow through by totally ending *all* contact. There's no benefit whatsoever in remaining connected in any way. You continue to dishonor your marriage by contact with your affair partner, and it only causes more pain for everyone.

Be prepared for the fact that your long-term lover may not go quietly. She may repeatedly violate your no-contact boundary via technology or (worse) in person. Stay firm. Unless you lied to her about being married, you have no obligation to this woman. (Even if you told her you were single, your responsibility toward her ends when you tell her the truth.) As surprising as it may sound, "kindness" isn't a helpful approach. Consistently and clearly restate your decision, if necessary, then stop responding if she contacts you. Change your phone number and email address if you need to. (You should already have unfriended her on social media.) If things get really difficult, you may need to involve your therapist or some other trusted advisor who can relay your desire to save your marriage and to live with integrity moving forward, which means ending the affair no matter how painful that may be.

Further, expect that you will grieve over the loss of your affair partner. Healing is painful, and loss is hard, even when you believe it's the right thing to do. Don't be fooled into thinking your grief is a sign you've made the wrong decision. It's just a predictable and normal consequence of your cheating. And hopefully you already know this next point if you've read this far, but don't be idiotic enough to think your wife will understand you pining over your affair partner. Find a trusted friend who can hear and hold your grief, and put on your best face for your spouse.

Questions for Reflection

1. Pushing aside all momentary anger and frustration, how do you really feel about your relationship with your wife? Or try the question this way: What would it be like for you to say goodbye to your wife and know that you will rarely or never see her again?

2. If you are choosing to stay in your marriage, how do you feel about the fact that your relationship will be different from now on—possibly better, but definitely different?

3. If you're ending a meaningful relationship with an affair partner, ask God to provide for her care and wellbeing. Every time you think of her or feel pangs of grief, entrust her to a loving God and ask God's grace to maintain your no-contact boundary.

CHAPTER SIX

SEVEN WAYS YOU CAN MAKE A BAD SITUATION WORSE

"I'm not upset that you lied to me; I'm upset that from now on I can't believe you."
—Friedrich Nietzsche

Edwin, a thirty-seven-year-old schoolteacher, was caught cheating. His wife, Elena, learned that he'd been having an affair with the mother of a former student when the other woman called Elena to spill the beans, hoping to break up the marriage and have Edwin to herself. Edwin initially denied the affair, even though it had been going on for almost three years, and he pretended that the other woman was simply disturbed. Later, after much questioning by his disbelieving wife, he finally admitted that he'd been sexual with the woman on one occasion. But he insisted that it was only one time and he'd ignored the woman ever since.

However, Edwin's history of text messages, e-mails, and phone calls—uncovered during some typical fear-driven detective work by Elena—painted a very different picture. When she confronted him with this proof, he tried to calm her down by insisting that the other woman meant nothing to him. He also claimed that he had only ever cheated with this one woman. Yet just a few weeks later

Elena uncovered a couple of hidden dating apps on his phone, which revealed that he had cheated with dozens of women and, even worse, had continued this behavior even after she discovered the first affair.

To appease her fury, Edwin surprised Elena with a beautiful new ring—a diamond wedding band, no less. He said he was sorry she was so hurt and wanted to renew their wedding vows as a fresh start. When Elena refused (strongly and with language he had never heard her use), Edwin said she wasn't being Christian by refusing to forgive him after he said he was sorry. She wouldn't budge and insisted he leave *right now*! Edwin responded by storming out, but not before saying, "I always thought you were hung up about stuff. At least now I know for sure you expect me and everything about us to be perfect. If you can't accept me like I am, then we're better off apart. And don't expect any alimony!"

First, Do No Harm

Perhaps you're familiar with the Hippocratic Oath, originally an ancient Greek medical text requiring physicians to uphold specific ethical standards. The original version reads, in part, "With regard to healing the sick, I will...take care that they suffer no further hurt or damage." The modern version, penned in 1964 by Louis Lasagna of Tufts Medical School, reads in part, "Most especially, I must tread with care." Both forms of the oath can essentially be summed up as, "First, do no harm," a mantra that is commonly used as a guiding principle by modern physicians and caregivers.

We mention this principle here because healing from infidelity has a similar guiding tenet: at minimum, do no more harm. However, if you're like most cheating men, the odds that you'll fulfill that ideal are slim. In fact, you're likely to make all sorts of mistakes as you try to heal your relationship, no matter how sincere you are. This chapter is written with the hope that you might develop an understanding of the most common mistakes that cheating men make after their infidelity is discovered. Better yet, we hope you'll recognize and avoid these pitfalls before they occur—unlike the hapless Edwin, who did basically everything wrong.

There are seven things you can do to make your current situation worse:

1. Continue to cheat.
2. Continue to lie, tell partial truths, and keep secrets.
3. Put the blame on someone or something other than yourself.
4. Apologize and then expect or demand immediate forgiveness.
5. Try to buy forgiveness.
6. Use aggression and threats.
7. Try to calm your spouse down.

Continuing the Infidelity

We're starting the list with the most obvious thing you can do to plummet from a status of bad to horribly, terribly awful. It goes without saying that you must quit being unfaithful, right? It's like us telling you that four pitches out of the strike zone puts the batter on first base. It's just very basic information. However, we're including this standard because a frighteningly large percentage of men (including Edwin, in the example that opens this chapter) just can't seem to stop cheating, no matter the consequences. In this way, some cheating men are like drug addicts: they lie, cheat, and keep huge secrets, all in the service of continuing their behavior. And they do this even after their infidelity (or part of it, anyway) has been uncovered and their world is crumbling around them.

It wouldn't surprise us if you confessed that you're feeling a strong urge to return to cheating *right this moment*, even if you've stopped and fully intend to stay stopped. And we get it. After all, the high of illicit sex is intoxicating and very hard to let go of. There's an immediate and potent short-term payoff. It's possible you're worried that your life will be mundane and boring without this thrill. Or maybe your spouse is being particularly vengeful and unpleasant in response to your cheating, and you think that her nasty behavior might be a reasonable justification to go back to it at least one more time.

Sex Addiction

Some (but not most) men who cheat are sexually addicted. For them, cheating is part of a larger pattern of compulsive sexual behavior that is engaged in regardless of consequences, and usually in an escalating pattern. In such cases, stopping the infidelity isn't likely to occur without outside assistance of some sort. Just as alcoholics and drug addicts go to rehab centers, Alcoholics Anonymous, and Narcotics Anonymous for help, sex addicts need similarly specific, often intensive treatment. Those who are sexually addicted are best helped through treatment from certified sex addiction therapists (CSATs) and social support in Twelve Step sexual recovery groups like Sexaholics Anonymous, Sex Addicts Anonymous, Sexual Compulsives Anonymous, and Sex and Love Addicts Anonymous.

If you think you might be sexually addicted, we urge you to seek assistance, education, and support for this issue. You might start with Rob's book, *Sex Addiction 101*, which explains the basics of that issue. More information on sexual addiction, useful to both addicts and betrayed partners, can be found at SexandRelationshipHealing.com and www.RobertWeissMSW.com. You might also research Bethesda Workshops, the ministry Marnie directs, which provides four-day intensive workshops for both sex addicts and partners (separately first, then they can return as a couple). See BethesdaWorkshops.org.

As we discussed earlier, if there has been an emotional component to your cheating, as with a long-term affair or even regular booty calls, letting go can be difficult—primarily because you care about the other woman and don't want to cause her pain. You might even decide that you can surreptitiously stay in contact, continuing the relationship but being a little more careful from now on. In other words, if you're emotionally attached to the other woman (or women), you may have a strong desire to continue lying and cheating, but to "do it better" this time around. If this is your thinking, please go back and re-read our impassioned statements near the end of the previous chapter about not maintaining contact with an affair partner.

Staying in contact with an affair partner and continuing to lie about it will only make things much, much worse. Even if your significant other initially believes your lie that the infidelity is over, she will inevitably find out the truth. Your continued breach of relationship trust will cause her incredible pain and anguish—much more than what she has experienced already. It often is enough to turn her away from you permanently. Before you continue cheating, we strongly advise you to think this idea through to its logical and extremely unpleasant outcome.

If you're determined to continue cheating, please man up and tell your wife now, and accept the consequences that will likely result. At least that admission has the integrity of being truthful.

Continuing to Lie, Tell Partial Truths, and Keep Secrets

Continuing to be dishonest relates to the preceding pitfall, but it deals with much more than ongoing sexual infidelity. It also involves a pattern of lies, cover-ups, partial admissions, and outright secrets about both past and current behavior of all types, including behavior not related to sex or romance. Aside from continuing the infidelity itself, ongoing lies, partial truths, and secrets are the easiest (and most potent) way to derail the process of saving your relationship.

A lot of the time, both outright lies and lies of omission occur because you don't want to hurt your wife anymore, and you think that what she doesn't know can't hurt her. Therefore, you tell her that your cheating occurred only once, or that you almost cheated but didn't, or that it didn't mean anything, or that you didn't have intercourse when you really did. Later, when caught red-handed in a deception, you admit to that specific incident and that one only. Regarding everything else, you continue to deny, deny, deny.

Essentially, you cling to the belief that you needn't fully disclose your past behavior and you "deserve some privacy" in the present. The problem with this approach is that it fails to incorporate your spouse's point of view. She likely needs to know the full truth about your past infidelity, and she will definitely need full transparency about your actions in the current moment. Without these concessions, she won't be able to heal, and trust will not be restored. Of course, neither of you wants to experience the pain that comes with full disclosure and ongoing transparency, but your relationship is likely to be doomed without those things.

Jumping the Gun on Disclosure

Sometimes men make the mistake of fully disclosing everything they've done too soon. Occasionally this is because the man's spouse has said she wants to know it all, and she wants to know it now. Other times, the man is thinking more about himself than his partner, and wants to get things off his chest to clear his conscience. Either way, making a full disclosure without the assistance of an experienced and knowledgeable therapist, preferably a couple's therapist or a similarly trained member of the clergy, is not recommended. In fact, unsupervised disclosure could easily lead to the end of your relationship.

The basics of disclosure are discussed in the next chapter and in an addendum at the end of the book. For now, we'll simply say that if your mate asks to know everything about your cheating, it's best to tell her that you aren't ready to provide full disclosure—not because you're unwilling to tell her, but because you want to make sure that you both have proper support and direction first. Then you should clearly state that you will tell her everything she wants to know, and sooner rather than later, but you want to do so with the assistance of a couple's counselor. Usually, if your spouse knows that she'll hear the truth at some point, preferably on a set date, she'll be patient. But don't ask her to wait more than a month, because that delay would be torturous and unfair to her.

Putting the Blame on Someone or Something Other Than Yourself

Externalizing blame (making the problem someone else's fault) is one of the most common tactics cheaters use to rationalize and justify their actions. While actively cheating, for example, you might have told yourself, "If my wife hadn't gained twenty pounds after we had the kids, I'd still find her attractive and I wouldn't be so interested in other women," or, "If she wasn't such a cold fish, I wouldn't be searching for hot sex elsewhere." Unfortunately, this tendency toward externalizing blame may continue even after your cheating is discovered. It typically crops up when your spouse seems exceedingly angry for no apparent reason. At such times you may find yourself thinking or even saying things like the following:

- "The way you're acting, who could blame me if I went out and cheated again? When will you just let this go so we can move on with our lives?"

- "Why are you so upset when I've told you a hundred times that it was only meaningless sex? You just don't seem to hear me when I tell you that I love only you."
- "You're so controlling now, and you watch every move I make. I feel like I'm five years old and you're my mother. You're driving me crazy and pushing me away with all of this insanity."

Here's our response to these and similarly understandable attitudes: Tolerating your spouse's anger and demands, while not blaming her for them, is what being in the doghouse is all about. It's not fun, nor should it be. If you want to get out of the doghouse and back into life with your significant other, you're going to have to earn that right. And that means accepting responsibility for what you've done. You cheated, and now your spouse is in pain and acting exactly the way a traumatized person typically behaves. Blaming her for your current predicament is ridiculous. No matter how much weight she gained, no matter how little sex she's had with you, no matter how moody or kid-focused she's been, she did not make you cheat. Cheating was your choice, not hers.

This means that when your wife can't let go of her anger, you can't look at her and say, "If you would just forgive me, then everything would get better." First, that's not true. Second, a statement like that, in which you're shifting blame onto her, will either make her angrier than she already is, or it will further traumatize and distance her. It's like getting whistled for an obvious yellow card foul in soccer, screaming at the referee about it, and then getting another yellow card, which means you've now got an automatic ejection. You've gone from bad to worse and gotten yourself tossed from the match because you blamed the wrong person, who rightfully took offense. In short, blaming your mate for *your own decisions* is extremely counterproductive if you want to heal your relationship and grow as a man.

Apologizing and Expecting or Demanding Immediate Forgiveness

Many men get upset about the fact that their wives aren't acknowledging their efforts at restoring trust. They say things like, "Doesn't she understand that I'm doing everything I'm supposed to be doing? I've stopped cheating and I'm taking responsibility for what I did. What more does she want?" However, as your spouse sees it, the fact that you're finally behaving the way you promised you would when you initially committed to monogamy is hardly cause for celebration. Nevertheless, in frustration, you may find yourself demanding that she acknowledge your hard work and progress by being a bit softer and more loving (and maybe even initiating sex with you)—all the stuff that typically comes with a trusting relationship. But the simple truth is that you no longer have a trusting relationship because you cheated and lied and kept important secrets.

Please hear us when we tell you this, because it's very important: Expecting your wife to be more loving just because you've stopped misbehaving for a few weeks is a bad idea. And if you try to see things from her perspective, you'll understand why. To her, you finally becoming honest and faithful doesn't exactly merit a pat on the back, because you were supposed to be honest and faithful all along.

If you still find that you need some positive reinforcement, consider it high praise that your partner is willing to speak to you after everything you've done to hurt her. If you want something more tangible, it's best to seek your "Attaboy!" elsewhere, perhaps from a friend, a family member, a support group member, a clergyperson, or your therapist.

If you're expecting immediate forgiveness from a woman you profoundly betrayed only a few weeks or months ago, simply because you've told her that you're sorry and it won't happen again, then you need to think again. Expecting her to let you off the hook that easily is just not realistic. Yes, you do deserve acknowledgment for working hard towards change, but not from your spouse. At least not yet.

Trying to Buy Forgiveness

One of the most common mistakes cheating men make when trying to win back a betrayed spouse is attempting to buy their way out of the doghouse with flowers, dinners, trips, jewelry, and other gifts. *This doesn't work.* Your spouse will probably accept the gift, and she might even say thank you, but she's not going to forgive you just because you bought her something nice. And she might reject your gift altogether, throwing it back at you and walking away in tears.

Gifts, no matter how expensive, don't undo the trauma wrought by infidelity. They never have, and they never will. Still, lots of men try this tactic. (Recall, for instance, Kobe Bryant and the $4 million diamond he bought his wife, Vanessa, after she learned about his cheating.) Be assured, this is not the route out of the doghouse. Saying you're sorry and then giving your spouse a romantic gift won't restore relationship trust or earn forgiveness. Moreover, your gift will forever be tainted because your mate will always associate it with your betrayal.

> Note: A variation on trying to buy forgiveness occurs when you use seduction, regret, lies, partial disclosure, good behavior, or any other form of manipulation to obtain forgiveness and keep your relationship. Understand that your significant other doesn't want you to buy her off (unless she wants to clean out your bank account). Instead, she wants you to be a man who understands what she's feeling, cares about those feelings (even if they are mostly anger directed at you), and behaves in ways that cause her to feel loved, valued, and adored instead of cheap, used, and abandoned.

Using Aggression and Threats

Sometimes cheating men get sick of their partner being so angry, and in response they get aggressive. The most common ways involve emotional and/or financial threats, like the following:

- "If you don't like my cheating, then maybe we should get a divorce. But don't count on some big payout from me."
- "If you want me to support you and the kids, I'm perfectly happy to do that. But you're going to have to get used to me stepping out with other women."
- "I'm not leaving, but I'm not limiting myself sexually, either. You're just going to have to live with that if you want to stay together."

Men who use aggression and threats in this way seem to think that the best defense is a good offense. It isn't. If you try this approach it's possible that you'll successfully bully your wife into submission—temporarily. More likely, however, you'll drive her further away. And if she does give in to your bullying, is that really the kind of relationship you want? Do you want your wife to stay with you only because you bullied her into it? You'll never have her respect, much less re-earn her trust with threats. What happened to your understanding of heart change?

Trying to Calm Her Down

If you want to watch your significant other really lose her temper, wait until she's already upset and then try to calm her down. Say something like, "Honey, relax. This isn't a big deal. You know I love you, and I always have. You're overreacting." Then you should probably duck and cover—because that's what you do when a tornado is heading your way, right?

Please trust us when we tell you that your spouse won't like it if you try to diminish (i.e., invalidate) her emotions. Sure, if you work hard enough, you might be able to calm her down a little bit, but it won't last, and it certainly won't fix your underlying issues with relationship trust. Besides, you are rightfully in the doghouse. Your wife's anger was caused by your actions. If you hadn't cheated and lied, she wouldn't be angry. So maybe you should just let her be angry, and be glad that she still cares enough to have strong feelings about you. Know too that a big part of her healing process is being able to express how your actions have affected her, and you need to live with that truth, no matter how awful it feels.

Perhaps more important, accepting your significant other's anger, sadness, disappointment, and hurt by letting her fully express it tells her that you care about her and your relationship enough to just sit there and take it. In this case, the best action you can take is no action at all, except perhaps to validate what she's feeling.

Questions for Reflection

1. Have you engaged in any of the seven pitfalls listed in this chapter? If so, which ones? How did your spouse respond?

2. Your wife is on an emotional roller coaster. It's helpful if you have a few kind and empathetic responses you can turn to in these difficult moments. Below are three common statements from betrayed wives. For each statement, come up with an empathetic response.

   - Your mate: I hate you and everything about you. I can't even look at you right now.
   - Your response:

   - Your mate: I know you're thinking about her. How can you do that when I'm right here in the room with you?
   - Your response:

- Your mate: You said you'd be home at 6:00. Now it's 6:30. Were you out cheating again? And no matter what you say, how am I supposed to trust your answer?
- Your response:

CHAPTER SEVEN

YOUR WAY OUT OF THE DOGHOUSE

> "The truth," Dumbledore sighed. "It is a beautiful and terrible thing, and should therefore be treated with great caution."
> —J. K. Rowling, *Harry Potter and the Sorcerer's Stone*

Healing is Never Pain-Free

You may recall that we began the preceding chapter with a brief discussion of the Hippocratic Oath, and noted that it can be summed up as "First, do no harm." Then we suggested that this pledge should be your mantra from now on. However, this doesn't mean that relationship recovery will be free of pain and hurt. In fact, what comes next is likely to be quite painful for all concerned.

If you're reading that and thinking, "Holy cow!" (or what comes from the back end of a cow), we totally understand.

Really, we do.

Let's return to medical doctors and their use of the Hippocratic Oath. All doctors are taught that in order to do long-term good, their actions may initially cause distress, pain, and even illness in their patients. Despite this reality, doctors' painful choices are carried out intentionally—with the sole goal of healing. Consider, for instance, oncologists (cancer doctors). These physicians often choose to treat their patients with radiation, chemotherapy, or other procedures and medications that cause all sorts of distress and discomfort. In fact, many cancer survivors will tell you that the treatment felt worse than the disease. Yet doctors proceed and patients go along because they know they're working toward a greater good: remission and recovery.

The list of medical reasons for ignoring the "first do no harm" tenet is actually pretty lengthy. Think about any surgery at all: "You want to drug me until I pass out, slice me open, and do *what?*" Nevertheless, people do agree to such procedures when they understand and accept the goal of healing.

In many ways, recovering from infidelity is the same. You, your wife, and your relationship will occasionally experience deep stress and pain as you heal. Even if you approach this process with the best of intentions, determined to cause your significant other no further pain, you won't succeed. She will ask you for more information about your cheating, you'll need to tell her the truth about some secret you've been keeping, you'll make a mistake and forget to check in with her when you promised, you'll run into an old flame and have to share that with her, etc. All are painful.

You might want to brace yourselves for a bumpy ride.

A Few Ground Rules

As you begin the process of rebuilding relationship trust, we strongly suggest the following to both you and your spouse:

- Put your relationship into a safe harbor during the early stages of relationship renewal. You and your wife should agree to not make any major decisions (such as divorce or legal separation) while you are working to rebuild trust and heal the relationship. As therapists, we typically recommend couples commit to a full year of this safe harbor, although many balk at that timeframe. In such cases, we suggest three to six months as an alternative, which nearly always seems more manageable. Then, at the end of that safe period, if the pair is making progress, we'll suggest they commit to another three to six months of relationship safety.

- During the process of healing, you and your spouse should put your primary needs for emotional support on friends, family, pastors, therapists, and people you have met in support groups rather than on each other. This shift is important because you're both going through a tough time and need emotional support, but you can't effectively provide it to each other at this time. (It's very difficult to seek and accept emotional support from the person you are most upset with.) Basically, the current lack of trust between you and your spouse temporarily prevents or at least diminishes the feelings of mutual support you once had. Whatever you do, do *not* reach out to a former affair partner or girlfriend.
- Take a time-out from sex, even if right now it feels like the best sex the two of you have ever had, and even if it makes your partner worry that you'll turn to other women because you can't be sexual with her. The reason for temporarily halting sex is simple. *Your spouse does not trust you right now, and there is no reason anyone should have sex with someone they don't trust.* Even if sex feels like temporary relationship glue, you need to understand that it's going to take more than that adhesive to grow and heal together.

These suggested guidelines won't prevent you and your mate from experiencing pain and emotional discomfort as you work to regain trust. What they can do is provide a bit of a cushion and soften the landing if either of you spirals downward. In other words, these cautionary measures won't prevent pain, but they can certainly diminish the impact.

Rigorous Honesty

If you want to get out of the doghouse, you'll have to rebuild relationship trust. And let us again be clear here: Relationship trust is not automatically rebuilt just because you stop cheating, nor is it rebuilt because you manage to stay stopped for a certain amount of time. Instead, relationship trust is regained through consistent and sometimes painful *actions* engaged in over time. Thus, you'll need to make a commitment to living differently and abiding by certain relationship boundaries. Perhaps the most important boundary is *ongoing rigorous honesty* about pretty much everything, all the time, from now on. This commitment means that you need to fearlessly tell the truth no matter what, starting right now, even when you know it might upset your mate.

When you're rigorously honest, you tell your significant other about everything, not just the stuff that's convenient or that you think will hurt her the least. There are no more lies and no more secrets. With rigorous honesty, *you tell the truth and you tell it sooner.* You keep your spouse in the loop about absolutely everything: spending, trips to the gym, gifts for the kids, issues at work, the need to fertilize the lawn, and, oh yeah, any "interactions" that she might not approve of. If your spouse would want to know, then you must voluntarily tell her. Period.

Thoughts vs. Actions

Rigorous honesty is more about your behavior than your thoughts. For instance, if you slip up and have a conversation with an old affair partner, you should tell your spouse, and the sooner the better. However, if you merely think about the fact that you'd like to call an old affair partner, you should talk about this with your therapist, pastor, or a close friend who knows about your cheating and is supportive of your healing process. To state it another way, if you think about it but don't do it, you still have to talk about it, but you should do so with someone other than your spouse. If you actually do it, however, then you have to tell your mate.

Rigorous honesty involves a spiritual paradox: You must be willing to lose the relationship by telling the complete truth if you have any hope of keeping it. Truth must become your most important and highest priority. Beyond the core truth of remaining fully faithful, recognize that women tend to view life and relationships much more holistically than men; therefore, even little white lies are out of bounds, no matter what your reasons are for telling them. If your wife catches you in a little white lie, it's predictable that she'll amplify that dishonesty to *everything* you say, and she will therefore assume that you're also telling big lies. So, when your mate asks if her favorite pants make her butt look big, you had better answer honestly. And when she asks how much money you spent on coffee this morning, you should answer to the penny.

You also need to understand the difference between *active* and *passive* truth telling. Active truth telling means you get honest with your significant other without her prompting you. If there's something you think she might want to know, you volunteer that information, and you do it sooner rather than later. Sure, she might get angry about whatever it is that you did, but she'll be a lot angrier if she finds out that you did it and then tried to keep it secret. With active truth telling you become fully transparent about every aspect of your life. Your spouse doesn't have to guess, make up stories that explain your behavior, ask probing questions, or play detective because you are actively disclosing the truth no matter what.

Passive truth telling forces your wife to do the work. With passive truth telling, even if she already knows or suspects that you're doing or have done something she might not like, you wait for her to ask you about it. And when she does, you tell the truth about what she asked, but you don't volunteer other pertinent information. Instead, you withhold this other information—while probably telling yourself that what she doesn't know can't hurt her. You might also try to convince yourself that you're not a liar because you answered her questions (more or less) truthfully. However, failing to disclose fully is just another form of lying. Believe us, that's certainly how your mate sees things. Passive truth telling won't help you to rebuild relationship trust. Furthermore, it will annoy the living daylights out of your wife.

Let's think back to our windows and walls analogy. When you actively and voluntarily tell the truth, you create nice big transparent windows that your partner can easily see through. When you passively tell the truth, you create little translucent windows through which she can only see blurry shadows and outlines of your life. This darkness, of course, invites her to use her imagination about what you might actually be doing. And can you guess the sorts of things she might imagine and how she'll react to these imagined fears and transgressions? We bet you can, and we bet you would rather she didn't. If so, all you need to do is tell the truth and tell it sooner.

Even when you've slipped up and done something that will disappoint and anger your mate, it's best to disclose the truth. If you can't bring yourself to reveal it today, then you need to tell her tomorrow at the latest. And you should let her know that you waited a day to tell her because you knew that she would rightfully be upset and you selfishly didn't want to experience that. While she might be angered by your delay, she will nevertheless appreciate your honesty.

Unfortunately, this process isn't as easy as it sounds. Ongoing rigorous honesty is often difficult and painful. You won't enjoy it, and your significant other won't enjoy it, either. However, it's a necessary part of healing.

When you practice rigorous honesty in your relationship, it's important that you not expect your spouse to immediately pat you on the back and thank you for your truthfulness. After all, you're in the doghouse, so that's not going to happen. And why should it, after you betrayed her, traumatized her, and made it difficult for her to believe *anything* you say? (Yes, we know we are repeating this and other principles, but most dogs require multiple training sessions to learn something new.) Over time, of course, if you truly are rigorously honest, she'll begin to appreciate this fact. Until then, you won't be able to predict or control her reactions, and you absolutely shouldn't try to do so. Your job is to keep your side of the street clean, day after day, until she finally starts to believe that you really are living your life openly and honestly.

How Secrets Leave Your Own Needs Unmet

One of Rob's clients, Sam, told him the following story about his belief that "what she doesn't know won't hurt her." As you'll see, the lesson Sam learned was that what she doesn't know actually hurts *him*.

Sam was at the office and had just finished lunch when his work-at-home wife, Ellen, called him, sounding upset and exhausted. It was summer, and their two wonderfully rambunctious sons, both under the age of ten, were out of school and home all day, bouncing off the walls and getting on Ellen's nerves. Having had enough, Ellen asked Sam to come home early, around three o'clock if possible, so she could go to a yoga class and then meet a few women friends for an early dinner and a movie. She told Sam that if she didn't get a break she was going to lose it, because she was completely drained both mentally and physically. Sam, sensing her distress, agreed to be home no later than three to play with and feed the boys.

Sam was happy to leave work early, but helping out around the house wasn't the only thing he had in mind. For quite some time, obviously without Ellen's knowledge, he'd been spending a fair amount of his free time (mostly during his lunch hour and on breaks at work) cruising hookup apps like Ashely Madison. However, because of his busy schedule he hadn't found much time to make the physical connections happen. This situation felt like a golden opportunity. He told his boss he had to leave work right away for a family emergency, even though he didn't need to be home for another two hours, and then he took off to meet a woman he'd sexted back and forth with several times. As far as he was concerned, this was the perfect plan. He had a legitimate excuse to leave work early, and he had two hours in which to act out sexually. Best of all, Ellen would be none the wiser.

The plan worked great, too. Sam had his sexual liaison and made it home with ten minutes to spare. Ellen thanked him and left for her yoga class. After that, Sam and the boys roughhoused outside, and then he made spaghetti (their favorite) for dinner. After eating, he and the boys played video games until Ellen returned.

At 9 p.m. Ellen walked in the door to find her family happy, engaged, and playful. She was relaxed and centered from her yoga class and time with friends, and she was more amused than upset by the mess that Sam and the kids had made. (No one had cleaned up in the kitchen after dinner, and video game boxes were all over the living room.) These little things didn't faze her because of how she *felt* about the family bonding she saw. Leaning over her husband's shoulders, she gave him a big hug from behind and whispered into his ear, "You know, you're the man I always wanted. Seeing you here with the kids, after giving me the time I needed for myself, just renews all my feelings of love and appreciation for you. I'm so glad I married you."

And there it was, something we all want and need simply because we're human: for the people we love to value and acknowledge us just for being ourselves. Honestly, who doesn't want and need to experience that at least occasionally? Being validated in this way, especially by those we love, is a basic human need.

Sadly, Sam wasn't able to hear or appreciate this valuable message. Instead, his wife's words brought feelings of deep shame and regret because Sam, unlike Ellen, knew the truth about where he'd been before this episode of domestic bliss. The minute Ellen walked through the door, Sam flashed back to the woman he'd cheated with, and he immediately felt awful because he knew how Ellen would feel if she knew what he had done. In his mind, he didn't deserve, nor could he accept, her kind words.

This reality is the hidden cost of secrecy and lies in our intimate relationships. While we may sometimes feel proud of our cleverness for getting away with all kinds of things our significant other will never know about, we also push ourselves away from the relationship intimacy that brings genuine happiness. Thus, our secrets—maybe not so clever after all—tend to keep us numb and self-hating, and they prevent us from receiving the love and appreciation we are given for the things we do right. When we know that we're keeping meaningful and potentially shameful sexual and romantic secrets from our mates, we can never fully accept the love that they give to us.

Can we get away with doing whatever we want in secret? In practice, maybe we can, at least for a while. In reality, not so much, because this kind of behavior comes at a steep emotional cost—to us. Lies block intimacy; it's just that simple. Proverbs 10:9 describes it this way: "Whoever walks in integrity walks securely, but he who makes his ways crooked will be found out" (English Standard Version). If you're full of secrets, it's impossible to be open and vulnerable with your wife. Neither can you accept her love, because deep down, she doesn't know the real you.

She Wants to Know Everything! And She Wants to Know Now!

It's understandable that your mate might want to know the complete history of your infidelity. In fact, she may want to hear about every graphic detail. Even worse, this desire to know everything could be mixed with periods of not wanting to know anything at all. Either way, your spouse has a right to know about anything and everything that has gone on during her relationship with you. After all, she's trying to figure out what you've done and how likely you are to do it again in the future.

It's probable your wife thinks that if she knows everything she'll feel a sense of control over an out-of-control situation. This belief is completely understandable. In fact, it's a perfectly normal reaction to almost any kind of traumatic experience, including the deep and incredibly painful emotional trauma caused by infidelity.

Generally, full disclosure about infidelity best occurs in the office of an experienced couple's counselor. (We've explained this process more fully in a separate section at the back of the book, and we urge you to read it. Please don't consider the material unimportant because it isn't part of a main chapter. This instruction is crucial; the topic is simply best situated at the end of the book.) That said, there could be a few things you need to disclose immediately, like the following:

- You must tell your partner right away if there are any risks to her health. Could you have an STD? If you do, could you have given it to her? (Don't assume that's not possible or likely.) If you've contracted an STD—or suspect that you have—and you've been sexual with your wife since then, you need to tell her, no matter how painful the disclosure. She deserves to know that she needs to make an appointment with her doctor.

- If you have kids and they might have seen or heard you acting out sexually (viewing porn, chatting with an affair partner, or even being sexual), you need to tell your mate about this reality right away. Protecting and nurturing your children is paramount, and your wife needs to know about any possible issues.
- If you have been sexual with anyone close to your significant other (or even someone with whom she has a casual but regular relationship, like the clerk at your local grocery store), you have to tell her about this up front. Otherwise, she might turn to that person for a sympathetic ear.

For things you must share immediately, here are few ground rules:

- **No graphic details.** While your partner may want every detail, and you likely remember every detail, giving her a clear image of you and another woman being sexual could send her packing. If you must, tell her general information about your behavior, but skip the gory particulars. If she demands more, you can insist on help from a therapist.
- **Give enough information for now, and only if she insists.** "I was having sex with strangers and occasionally prostitutes when I traveled. It was mostly oral sex, but there was some vaginal sex, too. I did this approximately X number of times since we've been together, and it's cost us X amount of money."
- **Avoid giving too much information.** "I love being with women with large breasts and big butts. With that type of woman I can do XYZ with her breasts and ABC with her butt. You don't know this, but I love doing XYZ and ABC with slutty women."
- **No more lying.** If you tell your spouse more lies or half-truths about your behavior, you'll destroy the process of healing before you even begin. Don't do this. If you do,

she will find out, and she likely will give up on the relationship and on you.

If your spouse is demanding that you give full disclosure right this instant, tell her you are more than willing to tell her anything she wants to know, but you want that process to be safe for you both—meaning disclosure with structure, boundaries, and guidance from a therapist. If she's insistent, suggest that you read together the section on disclosure at the end of this book. Included are some paragraphs just for her. Another helpful resource is a two-part podcast on the topic found on the Bethesda Workshops' website, which is the ministry Marnie leads for healing from sexual addiction. Visit www.BethesdaWorkshops.org.

As stated above, any attempts at full disclosure should occur *only with the support of an experienced couple's counselor.* Without this supervision, attempts at full disclosure can be disastrous. Even if it makes you feel better to come clean, it's unwise to just dump a bunch of painful information on your spouse. And this is true even if she's asked you to do it. As long as you are no longer cheating and you're telling the truth about your current behaviors, your spouse can wait on a full disclosure that takes place in a therapy setting. You shouldn't, however, delay full disclosure for more than a month. If your wife is demanding to know everything and you're serious about saving your relationship, make an appointment with a therapist and give disclosure as soon as possible.

It's possible your significant other will get exponentially angrier at your refusal to provide immediate, graphic disclosure. If you encounter this reaction, remember the heart principle. You have lied to her about the thing she holds most sacred (and believed you did, too). Your healthy boundary about guided full disclosure may seem, to her, like cowardly stonewalling or even more lies. Don't be defensive! Hear the pain behind your mate's demands. Say that you're sorry you've betrayed and hurt her so badly. Respond with gentleness and patience.

Realistically, if you're reading this book, some level of discovery or disclosure has already happened. You may be discouraged because you've blown it and already dumped all your dirty laundry with too many details—or maybe you insisted that you told her everything when that was a lie. Unfortunately, that's usually the way it happens during the early days a couple is dealing with infidelity. Don't despair. We repeatedly see that the best way to recover from a bad or incomplete disclosure is to engage in a healthy one. Despite the pain of hearing the complete truth, most wives appreciate your willingness to take this step. Perhaps surprisingly, most spouses even view it as a crucial step in the healing process.

To reiterate, you need to understand that even if your spouse thinks knowing everything will help her feel better, it usually doesn't. Sometimes, the more she knows, the worse she feels. However, full disclosure is still a necessary step toward rebuilding trust in most relationships, and you should therefore be prepared to give it. But please understand that if and when full disclosure is demanded, the best thing you can do for yourself and your relationship is to find a safe environment in which to give it, preferably the office of an experienced couple's therapist.

The Personal Benefits of Integrity

Disclosure isn't all about your significant other. You too will benefit. For starters, getting everything out in the open reduces the fantasy-driven allure of "the other woman." After all, forbidden fruit is exciting primarily because it's forbidden, exotic, and taboo. If you keep your cheating hidden, you're able to romanticize it in whatever way you choose—worshipping it as your perfect sexual prize while ignoring its flaws and the related consequences. Until you burst the bubble and dissolve the fantasy by talking about your behavior, you're likely to feel torn between your mate and your cheating.

When exposed to the light of day, infidelity rarely seems as enticing as when it was secret. The shortcomings and consequences are much easier to spot. In fact, after talking openly about their cheating, many men wonder what they ever saw in other women. They often realize that the women they've cheated with are not as pretty, smart, fun, and loving as their wives. However, this becomes clear only when the bubble is burst. Until then, old liaisons linger as obsessive fantasies, which causes other women to seem more attractive and appealing than they really are.

Other benefits of full disclosure include the following:

- **Reduced stress.** Making up lies, remembering them, planning for duplicity, covering things up, maintaining multiple online profiles (which must be kept secret from your spouse), hiding your spending, and other aspects of developing and maintaining sexual relationships outside your marriage all take a lot of effort. In fact, living this double life can be downright stressful. Sure, the drama of it all can be fun for a while, but eventually it starts to wear on you. Sometimes this erosion happens gradually and you barely notice it. However, when your lies are finally debunked and you have a chance to move forward with the truth—no longer worrying about what you told, to whom, and when—you're likely to feel as if a hundred-pound weight has been lifted off your shoulders.
- **An accurate narrative of your cheating.** You need this as much as your spouse does. You weren't lying only to your significant other when you were stepping out on her, you were lying to yourself. By disclosing, you debunk your internal lies and begin to understand how and why you crossed the line. Moreover, when you know the truth, you can develop the coping skills necessary to make sure you don't engage in similar behaviors in the future.
- **Reduced shame.** Keeping secrets about bad behavior creates a sense of shame and self-loathing. Most cheaters work very hard to push this aside, but they still sense it in a

nagging way. Usually, it's only after they're caught red-handed that these painful feelings bubble to the surface. Full disclosure (followed by a life of honesty) can alleviate and eliminate much of this discomfort.
- **Increased security.** Once your significant other has the truth, you understand that if she chooses to stay with you, she's made that decision in a fully informed way. Thus, you know that her decision to stay means that she truly does love you, and she believes in your ability to grow and heal. This realization will help you to feel better about yourself and your relationship.
- **Intimacy and true emotional connection.** Disclosure followed by honesty is the road to intimacy, the cornerstone of a healthy, enjoyable relationship, and an important fulfillment of your covenant with your mate. When you are honest with your wife, you create the possibility of a true partnership—an adult-to-adult relationship built on mutual trust, sharing, and enjoyment. Think about the windows and walls analogy. Disclosure tears down the walls that you built between you and your spouse, and it opens up some great big windows that allow you to fully see each other. At the same time, it creates healthy walls between you and your past affair partners.
- **Deepened relationship with God.** Most significantly, disclosure of your wrongs deepens your most important relationship: the one with God. You hide from God, too, when you cover up your cheating. You fear God's disapproval, rejection, condemnation, and abandonment. Yes, God does disapprove, because you've broken a God-ordained spiritual covenant as well as a personal and physical one. But God doesn't reject, condemn, or abandon you! God already knows your failings and loves you fully. In fact, God is the ultimate author of your healing and has compassion on those who struggle, including with sexual sin. Read Jesus' assurance in

Matthew 9: "It is not the healthy who need a doctor, but the sick" (verse 12). When you dare to fully confess your infidelity (ideally with the help of a trusted clergyperson or spiritual advisor), you open your heart to receive what you need the most: grace. In turn, forgiveness and grace deepen your relationship with God and your desire to honor it with your whole heart.

How Simple Lies Can End Relationship Healing

Eric sought therapy after his wife of eight years, Jeanette, discovered that he'd been going to local strip clubs and massage parlors. He said he was willing to go to any lengths to work on himself and make things right with his family. Jeanette said she wanted to stay with Eric, so she found a counselor, too—someone to help her work through her anger and grief related to Eric's extensive betrayal.

Eric attended individual therapy sessions and support groups with other cheating men. Through this process, he realized that his relationships with sex workers had nothing to do with his initial assumption that he was just really horny. In truth, he'd been leading a lonely life for quite some time, and he'd turned to sex workers for validation and attention. In therapy, he slowly came to realize that his chronic loneliness and sexual acting out stemmed from his childhood-to-adult feelings of "having to go it alone," and not from being a typical horny guy.

To be blunt, Eric had a very difficult childhood. Both of his parents were alcoholic, his father was mostly absent, and his mother was emotionally abusive. As a result, Eric learned he couldn't fully trust anyone, and as he grew older he determinedly became a completely independent person. As an adult, he took great pride in the fact that he didn't need help from others. For instance, he had built a successful business without going to college or accepting financial help from his parents or anyone else. Unfortunately, this same "completely independent" thought process made him blind to and dismissive of his (mostly unmet) emotional needs.

Because of this mindset, if Jeanette angered or disappointed him, he wouldn't talk it out with her. Thanks to his traumatic childhood he just wasn't able to trust anyone—not even his loving wife. So instead of talking to his spouse like most people might, he sought out other women and turned to them for the attention, validation, excitement, and distraction he desperately craved.

Eric did well in therapy and shifted his focus from work and self-sufficiency to self-care and emotional connection. He learned to make healthy recreation and downtime with friends and family a priority. As he began to feel more balanced and supported, his interest in seeking sex outside his marriage dissipated, but not his ongoing fear of losing his wife. Though he viewed both himself and Jeanette as independent and stable people, he was, in fact, quite needy emotionally, and he struggled with his healthy wife's seeming lack of dependence on him.

Meanwhile, Jeanette, who felt like her world had gone completely out of orbit due to her husband's sexcapades, just wanted her old life back. Though very angry and deeply hurt by Eric's infidelity, she was willing to work to save their relationship with one caveat: "I'm in, but only if he's done lying to me." With this boundary in mind, she and Eric slowly started to move toward reconciliation.

And then this seemingly simple mistake happened.

One day, about five months into their healing process, Jeanette had to leave early for work. Before leaving, she asked Eric to take out the trash, which Eric assured her he would do. Then, caught up in his own concerns, he simply forgot. That evening, as Jeanette walked through the door after a long day at the office, she casually asked, "Did you take out the trash?" Eric panicked. As silly as it might seem, he feared the anger and frustration Jeanette might express when she found out that he'd forgotten to do the one thing she had asked of him that day. So, rather than admit his mistake, he went into cover-up mode, looked Jeanette in the eyes, and said, very sincerely, "Of course I did."

A few moments later, while in the washroom cleaning up for dinner, Jeanette glanced out the window and saw Eric sneaking to the curb with the garbage he had forgotten to take out that morning. Unsurprisingly, Jeanette felt a knot of tension and anger grow in her stomach. For her, this seemingly small white lie represented something much greater. Suddenly, she could no longer trust a single thing Eric said or did.

Back in the kitchen, with no rancor or rage, she told Eric, "You lied to me again, and I'm done." She explained that she could not and would not allow any more lies and secrets in her life.

"But it's just the trash," Eric said. "It's not like I'm going back to strip clubs and fooling around on you. So why this reaction? You know I love you, right?"

Jeanette, feeling very calm, centered, and fully sure of herself, said, "I still love you, too. And I get that it's just the trash *to you*. But that's not where I'm at. I've been working very hard to regain my trust in you, and now I catch you blatantly lying to me yet again. I can't go back to that. And if you can't tell the truth about something as simple as admitting that you forgot to take out the garbage, how can I trust that *anything* you say or do is real?"

Two days later, with grace and sadness—and the support of her family and therapist—Jeanette left Eric and never came back.

> Note: This story isn't about men having to do everything perfectly to heal a broken relationship, nor is it about never making mistakes. Rather, it's about the power of lies and how even the simplest mistruth can finish a relationship that's on the brink.

Our point here is simple: Tell the truth and tell it sooner, even when you're afraid of the result. Do this even when you fear your significant other will be disappointed or angry with what you have to say. Remember, she's watching carefully for your lies, secrecy, and manipulations to return, because to her honesty is paramount. Your job is to do everything you can to regain her trust, so you need to be fearless (but never unkind) about whatever has happened. Whether you like it or not—trust us here—this is the path to healing your broken relationship. Being honest is far more important than looking good.

Another important point is the need to do deeper healing work when it's required. Eric's motivation to lie was driven by his powerful and pervasive childhood wounds and their resulting fears. It had nothing to do with his intention to deceive his wife, much less to return to cheating. Yet, he sadly hadn't admitted and dealt with his neediness and fear of abandonment. Don't quit before the necessary healing is done! If your infidelity is driven by deeper issues than immaturity, selfishness, or impulsivity, commit to a course of therapy with a professional trained in childhood trauma. Listen to that person and let her or him determine when you've completed your work, rather than relying on your own best thinking.

You've already cheated on your wife sexually. Don't cheat her out of the gift of being a healthy man in the holistic sense—one who is fully capable of partnering in a covenant relationship emotionally and spiritually.

Questions for Reflection

1. How do you feel about the concept of rigorous honesty? Do you think you can tell the truth and tell it sooner about absolutely everything, even the little stuff that doesn't seem to matter much? Why or why not?

2. Are you willing to fully disclose your sexual history to your spouse in the recommended way with the goal of staying together, or do you think there are things you can't tell her? If so, what are you afraid of telling her, and why?

3. Deep down, do you believe God rejects or abandons you because of your behavior? Put another way, do you think you can't re-earn God's favor with a return to fidelity? If so, reading Romans 8:1-17 may help. You might also consider talking with a trusted clergyperson or spiritual friend. Just take care to choose that person wisely. Sadly, many Christians are equally burdened with a works-based righteousness, rather than a relationship built on receiving the unfathomable grace of a loving God. Obviously, this deep spiritual work is beyond the nature of this book, but it's vital if you struggle with ongoing shame.

CHAPTER EIGHT

CREATING A COMMITMENT PLAN

> "Unless commitment is made, there are only promises and hopes… but no plans."
> —Peter F. Drucker

As you have probably figured out by now, there isn't much you can (or should) do to calm your mate down. You cheated and betrayed her trust, and now she is hurt, confused, and angry. And she's going to stay that way for a while, reacting in unpredictable fits and starts. She is on her own roller coaster journey, and you need to let her travel that path. In the interim, you can work on yourself and how you conduct yourself in your relationship (and elsewhere). This means setting limits on your sexual behavior and finding ways to stick to those limits.

Creating a Personal Fidelity Plan

It's time for you to create a personal fidelity plan that outlines which of your past sexual and romantic activities are no longer allowed, which are slippery, and some healthy things you can do when tempted to cheat again. After you've created this detailed plan, discussed it with others, and even shown it to your significant other, you're going to sign it, and contractually obligate yourself to abide by it. Think of this step as taking a vow of monogamy a second time, only this time you have a better understanding of what it means to keep it fully and how much is lost when you don't.

Creating your personal fidelity plan starts with a statement or list of the primary reasons you want to be faithful. Here are a few commonly stated goals:

- "I want to save my relationship."
- "I don't want to lie to my spouse anymore."
- "I want to uphold my marriage vows."
- "I don't want to hurt my partner or my kids anymore."
- "I want to live my life with integrity instead of feeling like a sneak."
- "I want to be the man God calls me to be—a guy who is just, kind, and walks humbly with God" (Micah 6:8).

Once your goals are clearly stated, you can take the next step in the creation of your personalized fidelity plan.

We recommend a plan that is three-tiered, consisting of a bottom line listing out-of-bounds behaviors, warning signs, and good stuff. Each of these tiers is described below.

The Bottom Line

The bottom line is your baseline definition of infidelity. Here you list the specific behaviors (not thoughts or fantasies) that qualify as infidelity in your relationship. This list will include all the ways in which you've cheated plus a general statement about infidelity that encompasses other methods of cheating. If you engage in any of these activities, you've cheated. A typical cheater's bottom line might include the following:

- I will not engage in sexual activity with any person other than my spouse. Things like oral sex, hand-jobs, and kissing qualify as sexual activity.

- I will not be sexual online with anyone other than my spouse. This includes webcam sex, virtual reality sex games, sexting, and flirting on dating or hookup websites and apps.
- I will not possess or access any dating or hookup apps or websites.
- I will not buy, look at, or masturbate to pornography.
- I will not flirt with other women. "Harmless flirting," with no intent to pursue a sexual encounter, still counts as flirting.
- I will not make or maintain contact (in person or digitally) with former lovers, girlfriends, dates, or hookups.
- I will not develop or maintain a deep friendship with another woman that involves sharing my hopes and dreams, fears and failures, disappointments (especially about my spouse or relationship), spiritual struggles, or similarly personal, intimate things. I will reserve those private exchanges for my wife.
- Other things that are off limits for me include: (List anything that is unique to you or your relationship. Examples might be going to lunch or having drinks alone with a female, traveling to business meetings together in the same car, etc.)
- In spiritual terms, my personal statement of fidelity is: (As an example, "I will devote myself to fidelity to God first and to shaping my heart and life to honoring God. I will love, honor, respect, cherish, and serve my mate with my whole heart, body, thoughts, and emotions." Write what works for you after some serious reflection.)

Warning Signs

Warning signs include the people, places, thoughts, fantasies, events, and experiences that might trigger your desire to pursue sex or romance outside your primary relationship. In addition to obvious potential triggers, such as logging on to the internet when alone, joining work buddies at a wild bar, or downloading a hookup app, this list should include things that might indirectly trigger your desires, such as working long hours with too little sleep, arguing with your spouse or your boss, keeping secrets (about anything), or worrying about finances. Here are a few items typically listed as warning signs:

- Lying and/or keeping secrets, especially from my spouse
- Skipping therapy or support group meetings
- Lack of self-care (not eating well, not exercising, not getting enough sleep, not taking time for fun)
- Attending parties and social gatherings, especially when my spouse isn't in attendance
- Business travel where I can disappear for a while and no one will know
- Unstructured free time (especially alone)
- Unresolved anger, frustration, irritability, and strong resentments—especially toward my spouse
- Not taking time to engage with my spouse on a one-to-one level
- Feeling slighted, ignored, or underappreciated
- Ignoring my spiritual practices or feeling disconnected from God

Good Stuff

The third tier of your plan lists healthy activities that will lead you toward fidelity and a better life. Essentially, these are things you can turn to when you feel tempted to cheat. These activities may be immediate and concrete, such as working out or painting the house, or long-term and less tangible, like getting a new job or taking classes. In all cases, your list should reflect a healthy combination of work, healing, recreation, and spiritual practices. Certainly things like going to individual and couple's counseling should be on the list. But you should also include fun things like spending time with friends, enjoying a hobby, and just plain relaxing. Here are a few items typically listed as good stuff:

- Spending quality time with my wife and kids
- Reconnecting with my male friends and working to strengthen those bonds
- Finding a new hobby, preferably something I can enjoy with my family
- Getting regular exercise to help with stress, mood, and body image
- Becoming more active in my church
- Working on my house and yard so I can feel proud of these things
- Going back to school to learn new skills
- Participating in the daily tasks of home such as cooking, cleaning, childcare, and gardening
- Joining a men's prayer or Bible study group
- Volunteering to coach my kids' teams
- Getting a (male) workout buddy
- Prioritizing my relationship with God

Every cheater and every relationship is different. Each person has a unique life history, relationship, and set of goals. Thus, no two fidelity plans are exactly the same. This means that activities that are deeply troubling for one cheater may be perfectly okay for another. For instance, some couples may agree it's fine for the man to masturbate (without fantasy or pornography) when he's away on an extended business trip; for other couples, this practice would be offensive.

This brings us to our next point: Don't create your personal fidelity plan on your own. Your spouse should have input, and so should your individual therapist, your couple's counselor, and anyone else who is playing an important role in the process of healing your relationship. And that's a good thing. The more thorough you are when creating your plan, the better.

Once your personal fidelity plan is finalized, you should sign it as an indication of your willingness to abide by it. Your spouse can keep a copy, and you should, too. It's also wise to share your plan with a trusted friend, your therapist, or a clergyperson—someone you trust to call you out on your behavior when needed.

Fidelity Plans: Top Tips

When first constructed, personal fidelity plans typically look airtight. However, despite their seemingly hermetic appearance, they usually aren't. Most cheaters who want to continue cheating can find (or build in) some wiggle room that lets them work around their boundaries. That's obviously not the way to rebuild trust and save your relationship. In recognition of this pitfall, we suggest that you keep the following tips in mind when you construct and implement your plan:

- **Be honest.** Creating an effective personal fidelity plan requires complete and brutal honesty on your part. Let's be frank here: If you're looking for ways to continue cheating, you'll find them. It's important for you to remember that the purpose of creating a fidelity plan isn't to justify and rationalize continued infidelity (or even watered-down versions thereof). Rather, the purpose is to end your cheating and the incomprehensible demoralization it brings.
- **Be clear.** If you lack clearly written boundaries, you'll be vulnerable to deciding in the moment that certain activities are "okay for now" even if they've been wildly problematic in the past. Impulsive sexual or relational decisions made without clear guidelines are what dragged you down in the first place, so it's best to not leave any wiggle room.

- **Be flexible.** A personal fidelity plan isn't necessarily set in stone. In fact, cheaters often spend a month or two (or even a year or two) with a set of boundaries, and then realize their plan requires adjustment. For instance, recent developments in digital technology (e.g., free porn sites, hookup apps, video chat services, and social media) have forced many former cheaters to revise their plans to include stronger boundaries about technology. That's fine, of course. The problematic changes are the ones you make the other way—deciding that something that was once off limits is now okay. Changing your plan isn't something you should do on your own. Making changes should *always* involve input from both your spouse and anyone else who is instrumental in your process of healing and rebuilding trust. Changes to a fidelity plan should never be made simply because a special situation presents itself and you decide, in the moment, to make a change. That isn't changing your plan, it's paving the road to continued infidelity.

More Boundaries to Consider

In addition to creating and following your personal fidelity plan, you and your spouse can agree on and implement any number of other boundaries. These might include the following:

- **The 24-hour disclosure rule.** The simple, sad truth is that you won't accomplish the process of healing and rebuilding trust perfectly. You just won't. You will screw up at some point, and you'll need to tell your spouse about it. Anticipating this reality, you can implement a boundary that requires you to tell her what happened, no matter what, within 24 hours. This practice gives you an opportunity to be honest and to talk about what you did, what led to it, and the precautions you'll need to take in the future. Understand that your spouse is allowed to be angry about what you did. You screwed up, and you'll have to accept her reaction. But at least you're being honest with her.

- **Amending lies.** If you're like most men who cheat, telling lies has become a habit. If this is the case with you (remember Eric, who lied about taking out the trash), perhaps you and your partner can agree that when you tell a lie, you have 24 hours to come clean without her getting angry about it. She can be mad about what you did, of course, but she'll extend grace about the fact that you initially lied to her about it—provided you fess up within 24 hours. After that, your fib is absolutely in play, and she has every right to scream and yell about it.

- **Addressing problematic drinking or drug use.** This is a big one for a lot of relationships. If you're a serious drinker or drug user, your significant other may want that behavior to cease along with your cheating. Frankly, it's a good idea. After all, alcohol and drugs inhibit your ability to make intelligent, rational, well-reasoned decisions (like the decision to not cheat even though the opportunity has arisen). If you are addicted to alcohol or drugs, you will find this boundary difficult, and you'll probably need outside assistance via inpatient treatment, outpatient treatment, and/or a Twelve Step recovery program.

- **Installing "parental control" software.** There are numerous products, most notably Net Nanny, designed to protect kids from inappropriate sexual content and contact in the digital universe. These products are equally useful for cheaters. They typically offer filtering and blocking (of problematic websites, apps, and contacts) as well as monitoring and reporting to a third party. Generally, this third party is your therapist or an accountability partner, rather than your spouse. If, however, your spouse wants to monitor your digital wanderings, so be it. In fact, your willingness to provide this level of access will go a long way toward rebuilding relationship trust.

- **Prove where you are and what you're doing.** Smartphones and their cameras allow you to easily have a video conversation or send a picture, which assures your mate that you're really stuck in a massive traffic jam, working out at the gym, or in your office later than you expected.
- **The ten-minute rule.** This one is pretty simple. You agree that if your wife phones you or texts you and you can't answer immediately, you'll respond within ten minutes no matter what, even if you're in the middle of an important business meeting. (If you actually are in a business meeting, you can say, "Excuse me, this looks like a family emergency." Even the stodgiest people will allow you to quickly step out of the room to handle the "emergency" without judging you for it.) This rule also applies to your mate. During the few minutes it takes you to respond, she agrees that she won't assume anything and won't get mad that you didn't answer right away. After ten minutes, however, all bets are off. (If you're going to be on an airplane or driving through an area without cellular service, you'll have to let her know about this in advance.) After more trust is rebuilt, she might be fine with you notifying her that you will be tied up doing XYZ at work from this time to that time, and she'll only contact you during that period if there's a significant need.
- **Full financial accountability.** If your spouse is interested in tracking how and where you spend money, as many betrayed women are, let her see your finances, both small and large. If you spent money on your cheating—and, let's face it, you almost certainly did—then becoming accountable for every penny you spend from here on out will help your significant other believe that even though you betrayed her in the past, you aren't doing so anymore.

In addition, your willingness to be an open book financially will help her understand that you're also being an open book with the rest of your life. (Remember, most women see the world holistically, so for them, honesty here signals honesty elsewhere.)

Fidelity Tools That Are Just for You

You'll be glad to know that not everything you do requires a conversation with your spouse. In fact, there are numerous personal tools you can utilize when you feel triggered toward cheating, and your mate won't need or even want to know that you've used one. She deserves to know about any actions that might hurt her, but hearing about every little thought that you didn't act on isn't helpful. And believe us, you will at least occasionally be triggered toward a return to infidelity. How could you not be, when our consumer culture is so thoroughly drenched in sex? The good news is that when you drive past a billboard advertising a nearby strip club, see a lingerie commercial or a movie with some explicit scenes, or run into a woman who reminds you of a woman you cheated with, there are plenty of highly useful tools at your disposal, including the following:

- **Your personal fidelity plan.** We generally recommend that reformed cheaters carry a printed or digitized version of their personal fidelity plan at all times. Not only does your plan provide clarity about which of your actions are and aren't acceptable in the moment, it also lists healthy alternatives you can turn to when tempted toward relapse.
- **Your accountability partner.** An accountability partner is a man with whom you can share your interior world—the inappropriate thoughts and temptations, and your frustration about the fact that your wife isn't patting you on the back every time you do the right thing and don't cheat on her, even though you could easily do so without her finding out. Ideally, your accountability partner will be

a friend who has overcome infidelity in his own relationship, but your therapist or minister will do in a pinch. The most important responsibility of an accountability partner is to talk you off the ledge when you're angry or feeling tempted to cheat.

- **The three-second rule.** No matter how much willpower you have, you aren't in control of the thoughts that pop into your head. What you can control is what you do with those thoughts once you become aware of them. Therefore, after recognizing that you're thinking about sexual activity with another woman, give yourself three seconds to turn away from that thought and focus on something else. Most men simply turn their thoughts to that woman being a real person (and not just a hot body), often by thinking of her as someone's mother, sister, wife, or daughter. You can also focus on who pitched game four of last year's World Series, what color you should paint the house, or the fact that your dog won't stop crapping in your flower bed. All you really need to do is think about something that doesn't involve cheating. You should be aware that unwanted sexual thoughts might pop into your head *ad nauseam*. This is especially likely if your cheating involved an emotionally connected affair. You'll get rid of one tormenting thought, and another will arrive almost immediately. In such cases, the three-second rule can be used repeatedly. It doesn't lose power. In fact, the more you use it, the better it works.
- **Bookending.** Most sexual triggers crop up unexpectedly. However, some can be seen well in advance. For instance, the office Christmas party is coming up, and the woman from accounting with whom you had an affair will be there. There's also an open bar, so everybody will be drinking and getting a bit loose. Instead of just going to the party and taking your chances, you can bookend the event. Before the event, you call your therapist or your

accountability partner and commit to fidelity, perhaps discussing plans to avoid any sort of cheating. After the event, you call the same person to discuss what happened, the feelings that came up, and what you might need to do differently next time. (Better yet, you skip the party altogether unless your wife will be there.)
- **Self-checks.** This is a way to gauge your mood and susceptibility to infidelity. The easiest way to go about this is to HALT, with HALT being an acronym for Hungry, Angry, Lonely, and Tired. (Some people use *anxious* rather than *angry*.) When you HALT, you ask yourself, "When is the last time I ate? Did I get enough sleep last night? Is there some conflict in my life that I need to resolve? Would a few minutes spent talking with someone who understands me help me feel better?" More often than not, a catnap, a protein bar, or a five-minute phone conversation will greatly diminish your in-the-moment desire to cheat.
- **Gratitude.** Reformed cheaters sometimes find that they're most tempted toward infidelity when they are feeling negative emotions (like anxiety, fear, shame, depression, or resentment). A great way to combat this is to write a ten-item gratitude list. A side benefit of this exercise is that it promotes happiness. In fact, as the amazing Brené Brown notes, gratitude and happiness are inextricably linked. According to her research (2012), grateful people tend to focus more on their strengths than their weaknesses, which makes them more hopeful, less stressed, and more likely to overcome major problems (such as infidelity in a relationship).

The tools listed above hardly represent the full kit. Keeping a journal, exercising, connecting with your therapist and/or your accountability partner, checking in with your family, developing healthy hobbies, praying, meditating, and just plain thinking things through are a few of the hundreds of other tools that you can use to combat triggers toward infidelity.

Questions for Reflection

1. What are your goals for your primary relationship, both short-term and long-term?

2. Are you willing to place limitations on your behavior as a way to heal and improve your relationship? If so, what are they? What might keep you from setting healthy boundaries? (Be honest.)

3. Do you feel grateful for your marriage and the woman with whom you share your life? If so, list ten reasons for this. Then list ten more.

4. Do you feel resentful for having to change your life to make your spouse happy? If so, write out what you resent and why.

CHAPTER NINE

EIGHT WAYS TO MAKE THINGS BETTER

"Integrity is doing the right thing even when no one is watching."
—C. S. Lewis

Making It Right

The preceding two chapters discussed what you can do to begin the process of getting out of the doghouse—embarking on a path of rigorous honesty and establishing (and sticking to) fidelity related boundaries. Once you've done those things, you've made a great start toward repairing your relationship and re-earning your spouse's trust. However, you're barely out of the starting gate in terms of making things right with her, and you're still looking at many months of (slowly decreasing) mistrust and emotional volatility.

The good news is that if you're rigorously honest and stick to your personal fidelity plan, you'll wake up one morning and realize that it's been several days or maybe even several weeks since your partner has blown up or acted as though she doesn't believe you.

Making it right with your mate is the second biggest area of fulfilling the heart change that's the core message of this book. Obviously, you had a heart problem when you cheated in the first place, and much of this book has focused on helping you understand that reality in three areas: *yes, you really were unfaithful; yes, it was absolutely devastating to your wife; and yes, you must completely stop cheating and lying.*

Now you're ready for the restorative part of healing, which involves taking specific positive steps. These actions speed up the healing process, and they discipline you (in the best sense of that word, which means "to teach") to be the man God calls you to be.

Eight actions of restitution and renewal are listed below:

1. Develop empathy for your spouse.
2. Learn to disagree in healthy and productive ways.
3. Instead of telling her you care, show her you care.
4. Always keep relationship trust in mind.
5. Anticipate potential hazards.
6. Don't forget about self-care.
7. Express gratitude to your spouse.
8. View love as a verb.

Develop Empathy for Your Spouse

The single biggest step you can take toward rebuilding relationship trust and a more intimate bond with your mate involves empathy. You're familiar with the word, of course, but most people lack a complete understanding of what it means. Empathy is the ability to understand and share the feelings of another sentient being. According to the Miriam-Webster dictionary, being sentient is perceiving and responding to sensations of whatever kind—sight, hearing, touch, taste, or smell. Sentient ultimately comes from the Latin verb *sentire*, which means "to feel," and this nuance is what's most important here.

Empathy is something that most women are naturally good at, and most men are naturally *not* good at. For instance, if your wife's best friend has been diagnosed with cancer, your wife will automatically feel the same emotional anguish as her friend, because that's how women are wired. Conversely, if your best friend has just been diagnosed with the same disease, you'll probably react with a desire to fix it, and you'll make suggestions on what he might do to get well. In other words, women typically deal with problems by sharing the emotional pain, while men deal with them by looking for a solution.

This doesn't mean that men don't experience empathy. They do. When they're playing softball and the pitcher takes a line drive to the groin, what is their first reaction? They automatically wince and say, "Ouch!" They feel the pitcher's physical pain, even though it didn't happen to them. That's empathy. Men are actually pretty good at empathy when it comes to physical pain. But they tend to fall short when it comes to the emotional stuff. Basically, when a man's significant other is feeling the emotional anguish caused by his betrayal, instead of empathizing (i.e., stepping into her shoes and feeling her pain), his natural tendency, as a man, is to look for a way to stop her crying. That's what guys naturally do.

As you read this you might be thinking, *I have plenty of empathy, so don't lump me in with the other insensitive jerks you normally deal with. I'm different.* If so, we'll just say (with the utmost respect and understanding) that if you truly had empathy for your spouse, you wouldn't have cheated. Instead, you would have thought, *Wow, I really want to have sex with this other woman, but I know that my wife would feel betrayed and hurt and would find it hard to ever trust me again.* And then you would have walked away.

Even though emotional empathy doesn't come automatically to most men, it can be developed with practice. And the more empathy you feel, the easier it is to understand and show patience with your wounded mate's sometimes erratic and seemingly inexplicable reactions to your cheating. When you really empathize, instead of blaming her or thinking that there's something wrong with her or feeling incredibly frustrated with her, you can start to understand what she's feeling and why she's bumping you along on her emotional roller coaster ride.

Deciphering your mate's thoughts and feelings isn't easy, of course, and you won't learn how overnight. Initially, you'll need to learn how she thinks and feels through open and honest communication coupled with a bit of trial and error. You'll have to consistently put yourself in her shoes and say things like, "I sense you're feeling some anxiety. Is that right? If it is, can you explain what you're anxious about? I really want to understand what you're feeling."

In general, however, you can bet that if she's behaving in a way that doesn't make any sense to you, she is likely feeling one or more of the following:

- Fear of further loss and abandonment
- Shame (feeling unworthy of love, as if the cheating were somehow her fault and she deserved it and can never expect anything better from you or anyone else)
- Self-doubt (fearing that whatever move she makes will be the wrong one)
- Anxiety (the constant fear that something bad is lurking around the corner)
- Worries about the future (related to finances, separation/divorce, or caring for the kids)
- Intrusive thoughts and mental pictures of your cheating

All these things are very natural reactions to traumatic betrayals by a loved one (i.e., you). Fortunately, as you learn over time to empathize with her fear, shame, self-doubt, anxiety, and whatever else she's feeling—when you're able to *feel these things with her*—it becomes much easier to understand and accept her ups and downs.

Learn to Disagree in Healthy and Productive Ways

As mentioned repeatedly throughout this book, being in the doghouse isn't fun. For starters, your partner gets angry with you for seemingly no reason, and there's little you can do to calm her down. For the most part, you just have to sit there and take it. And usually that's what she wants. Occasionally, however, your mate will want to argue with you. In fact, she might almost insist on it, no matter how hard you try to sit quietly. This is especially likely when you are being rigorously honest.

That seems unfair. You do the right thing, yet she still wants to fight. However, these disagreements aren't a bad thing. Believe it or not, arguments can evolve into deeper relationship intimacy. In addition, her desire to argue with you is a strong indication that she still cares about you. Think about it: Do you argue with people you don't care about, over topics you don't care about? Probably not. Her wanting to fight with you is a sign that she still cares about you and your relationship. The trick, of course, is learning to resolve these conflicts in ways that strengthen rather than diminish your relationship, which can be very difficult after you've cheated on her.

Sometimes when we have clients who seem to disagree and fight a lot without accomplishing much in the process, we present them with the following guidelines for respectful conflict resolution. We ask them to read the agreement, sign it, and take a copy home so they can work on resolving conflicts not just in therapy, but in the wider world. We suggest you read through these guidelines, and if they seem helpful to you, you can present them to your spouse as a way of turning potentially nasty arguments into meaningful and productive conversations.

Respectful Conflict Agreement

The purpose of this agreement is to create a safe and

intimate environment for conversations when we're in conflict. It offers a way to establish respectful guidelines and boundaries that allow for the healthy expression of emotions, and to ensure that both parties feel heard even if full agreement isn't reached.

- We agree that we are allies and on the same team.
- We agree to review this agreement weekly and before attempting to resolve any conflict. We agree to do our utmost to uphold this agreement.
- If either of us needs a time-out to cool off, we agree in advance that the first time-out will be for fifteen minutes. The person requesting the time-out agrees to say, "I need a time-out for fifteen minutes. I'm not leaving the discussion or the relationship. I just need a short time-out." That person then leaves the room and goes for a short walk or has a brief phone conversation with a supportive friend, and then returns on time to finish the discussion.
- We agree to limit discussions of loaded topics to twenty minutes. A timer can be used if either of us wishes it. When the time is up, if the conflict isn't resolved, we will agree to either continue the discussion for another twenty minutes or to schedule a later time to complete the conversation.
- We agree not to discuss loaded topics before 9:00 am or after 9:00 pm. (This can be adjusted depending on the couple's needs and lifestyle.)
- We agree that we won't engage in name-calling, we won't use offensive language, and we won't be emotionally abusive.
- We agree that we won't be physically abusive. This includes but is not limited to shoving, hitting, slamming doors, and breaking or throwing things. We

also agree not to engage in threatening behavior that we know our partner fears, such as threats of abandonment or exile. If either of us is in fear of the other, we agree to be honest about our feelings.
- We agree to identify the issue that needs to be discussed and to keep the conversation about that issue only. At the same time, we understand that the problem at hand may trigger, for one or both of us, a core issue from childhood or elsewhere in our past. When this occurs, we agree to differentiate between the present and the past as best we can.
- We agree not to attempt conflict resolution while driving, while in bed, during the workday, at a place of employment, when hostile behavior may escalate (such as after a few drinks), or when one of us is feeling low, vulnerable, tired, hungry, or otherwise not up to the task.
- We agree not to attempt conflict resolution in public or in the presence of family members (especially our kids). If conflict erupts at these times, we agree to acknowledge the upset feelings, and to set a time to discuss the issue.
- We agree to close a conflict resolution conversation with a couple-affirming prayer. (If the couple doesn't wish to engage in prayer, we generally suggest a couple-centered affirmation, such as, "We love each other, and we know that our differences and disagreements are a normal part of any relationship. We choose to not let them define us or cause us to doubt our love.")
- We agree to ask for help if either of us feels unable to remain respectful in our attempt to resolve a particular disagreement.

We enter this agreement willingly and lovingly.

Signature of Partner A:

Signature of Partner B:

The principles in this agreement probably seem relatively logical and straightforward to most readers. However, these common-sense guidelines can still be hard to follow. Because of this reality, we always stress the first item on the list: *We agree that we are allies and on the same team.* This principle is key for both you and your spouse. You need to understand that you shouldn't be fighting each other, you should instead be fighting the problem, whatever that might be. When two people agree that they're on the same team—the team that wants to make things better—strong disagreements tend to dissipate, and it becomes much easier to work together toward a common goal.

We also want to point out the final item on the list: allowing one or both parties to *ask for help* if and when conflict resolution goes awry. For some couples, especially those who are battling years of hurt and disagreement, this happens relatively often. No matter how hard they try to be on the same team, sometimes they need the impartial input of a third party (usually a therapist or clergyperson). However, with practice and commitment, even the most troubled partners can improve their communication and conflict resolution skills.

Show Her You Care

When you're making amends and seeking forgiveness, actions speak much louder than words. You can tell her a thousand times that you're sorry and that you really do love her. But after dealing with all your lies and secrets, she'll find it hard to believe your words. Your actions need to back you up. The following suggestions can help:

- Listen to what your spouse says and try to really hear it. Let it sink in. Try to see things from her perspective and to feel what she's feeling. More important, do this without becoming defensive or reacting with any other form of negativity. This response takes a lot of practice, and you won't always do it perfectly (especially at first). However, your wife will appreciate the effort you're making, and in time you'll get much better at it. If you're struggling, it's best to repeat back to her what you think you've heard, and allow her to guide and correct your interpretation to make sure you really do understand.
- Remember the dates and events that are important to her. You may not be focused on the anniversary of your first date, but if she has it on her calendar, you should put it on yours as well. This also goes for her sister's birthday, your child's school play, the neighborhood picnic, her night out with the girls, and any other event she values. Be sure to also notice dates like her mammogram or gynecological exam, which probably aren't on your radar as a big deal. But believe us (especially believe Marnie), these appointments are unpleasant under normal circumstances. After your cheating, they are especially emotionally painful.
- Spend time with her, preferably doing things she enjoys or helping her with tasks she doesn't enjoy. For instance, get up early and do the laundry while she's still sleeping. (And don't expect a gold star for doing it.) You can also ask her to join you on activities that you find fun, even though they might not be her favorite. When you do this, it's wise to tell her that you know this activity isn't at the top of her enjoyment list, but if she wants to come along anyway, you would be happy to have her company. If she chooses to join you, great. If not, at least you asked. It doesn't really matter what you do together, as long as she understands that you really do want to spend time with her.

Even if you implement the above suggestions imperfectly, your spouse will notice the effort you're making. Listening to her, making what's important to her important to you, and wanting to spend time with her all tell her that you really do value her and your relationship. As she sees you consistently doing these things, her anger will slowly ebb. She'll still have her moments, but they will gradually become less intense and less frequent.

Always Keep Relationship Trust in Mind

As mentioned throughout this book, you'll be in the doghouse until you repair relationship trust. To this end, you can implement the following tactics:

- Make rigorous honesty a way of life not just with your significant other, but with everyone. When she sees you being honest with every person you encounter, she's more likely to believe that you're also being honest with her. This means honesty in simple things, like correcting the amount when you've been given too much change, and big things, like owning up with your boss that you failed to return an important phone call in a timely manner.
- Keep your commitments. Suit up and show up when and where you say you will. Keep your promises to her no matter what, even if doing so is wildly inconvenient. If she sees you keeping your daily commitments, she's more likely to trust that you're also keeping your commitment to fidelity.
- Be patient. You can't rebuild relationship trust overnight. It's a process, and it takes both time and a considerable amount of conscious effort. Even worse, it's usually a two steps forward, one step backward process. You'll think you're doing great and she's finally coming around, but then something will upset her—you probably won't even know what—and it will suddenly feel as if you are back at

ground zero. This is normal. Don't get angry about it, and don't point it out to her.

- Understand that the new version of relationship trust you are building won't be as unconditionally accepting as the old version. As such, you'll need to maintain much tighter boundaries than before: calling if you're running late, admitting when you're wrong, and fessing up if you tell a lie or keep a secret. And you might need to maintain these new boundaries for a very long time. (Actually, consider these practices to be a forever part of your regular life. View them as part of basic integrity and consideration in a covenant relationship.)

It's hard to accept your mate's continuing distrust when you know that you're finally being rigorously honest about all aspects of your life. However, doing so is part of the healing process for you both. Over time, as you continually work to re-earn her trust, she'll come around. One day you'll wake up and realize that she hasn't questioned you in weeks. And that will feel incredible. Even better, because you had to work so hard to reestablish relationship trust, you're much less likely to break it again in the future.

Anticipate Potential Hazards

The process of healing from infidelity doesn't always go smoothly. In fact, many former cheaters will relapse at least once or twice. When this occurs, the best they can do is admit what they've done and amend their future behavior. With a bit of preparation, however, these setbacks can be avoided altogether, especially if you know the warning signs to keep an eye on.

The most common warning signs of a potential backslide are as follows:

- **Overconfidence.** "This is going really well. Maybe I have the problem licked and I can let my guard down."

- **Denial.** "See, I can stop cheating any time I want. Now that I've proved this, I can look at and flirt with other women like a normal guy."
- **Isolation.** "I can handle this on my own. I don't need to go to therapy and I don't need to be in constant contact with people who support what I'm trying to do."
- **Blame.** "If my wife hadn't gotten that new job that takes up so much of her time and energy, I wouldn't feel the need to go online to socialize."
- **Excuses.** "I know that being alone with my computer is a danger zone, but I need to stay late at the office to finish this important project."
- **Slippery Situations.** "The buffet at that Chinese restaurant across the street from where the prostitutes hang out (or where my affair partner works) is really good, so I'm going to have lunch there."
- **Minimization.** "I'm only looking at a little porn. It's not like I've gone back to having affairs."
- **Devaluating Feedback from Supportive Others.** "The people in my therapy group just want to control me. The stuff they want me to do might work for them, but they don't understand my situation."
- **Feeling like a Victim.** "I don't understand why I have to deprive myself when everybody else can look at porn and have webcam sex without fear or problems."
- **Rationalizing.** "It's okay for me to sneak around a little when I'm traveling for work. My fidelity plan doesn't count when I'm in a different state, right?"
- **Ignoring Previously Agreed-Upon Guidelines.** "I know I promised my spouse I wouldn't look at porn or flirt with other women on hookup apps, but what she doesn't know can't hurt her."

- **Feeling Entitled.** "I've been putting in double-duty at work, and nobody seems to appreciate the effort I'm making. I deserve a little something just for me."
- **Taking or Returning Calls, Texts, or E-mails from Former Cheating Partners.** "It's mean if I just ignore her. Anyway, what's the harm in just chatting?"

When you're faced with any of these warning signs, it is best to be honest about that right away with your therapist and/or an accountability partner. Talking about your temptations will greatly reduce their power and the hold they have over you. The good news is that you needn't share this with your spouse. In fact, she probably doesn't want to know about the occasional wandering thought. She's much more focused on the things you actually do.

Don't Forget About Self-Care

Sometimes men who've cheated on their intimate partners get so focused on repairing the relationship that they forget to take care of themselves. In the first few months of the healing process, this may be a reasonable response. Essentially, you feel so awful about your cheating that think you don't deserve any sort of external support, enjoyment, or personal fulfillment. Instead, you throw your entire self into repairing your relationship. And while this is an admirable objective, it's difficult to sustain and it's not healthy in the long run. Over time, the shiny new adventure of rebuilding your relationship turns into a chore from which you never get a break. When that occurs, your motivation inevitably wanes.

If this happens to you, don't fret. You aren't alone. In fact, at least half the men we treat for infidelity-related issues experience this to some degree. They become so focused on rebuilding trust and healing the relationship that they lose track of life. Beyond their job and the work of staying married, they are aimless, and this affects them emotionally and mentally.

When we encounter such men, we try to expand their focus by asking, "What do you want from life beyond your relationship?" Most of the time they're startled to realize that they have no idea. At that point we suggest they think about ways in which they can start to once again enjoy positive things beyond repairing and rebuilding their relationship. We typically ask these men to create a list of life goals beyond the development of sexual integrity.

One of Rob's clients, Gavin, created the following list and shared it during an individual therapy session:

- I want to be present in my life rather than tuned out and unavailable.
- I want to earn a promotion at work so I can be a better provider for my family.
- I want my spouse and kids to love and to trust me.
- I want to be truthful in all my affairs.
- I want to be a good person: a good neighbor, a good member of my community, and most of all a good family man and Christian.

Gavin was pretty pleased when he shared this list. Or he was until he heard the response, "Yes, that's all very nice. But what else do you want?" Unsurprisingly, Gavin was a bit frustrated with that answer. Rob asked, "Do you want to go on an amazing vacation? Do you want to join a softball team? Do you want to start a new hobby? Do you want to repaint your house? What about Go-Kart racing with your buddies from work?" Gavin admitted that a few of those options interested him. "So why aren't they on the list?" Rob asked. "All I see now is work, work, and more work. What about having some fun?"

Our point to Gavin (and to you) is this: If you're not going to have some fun and enjoy your life while you're in a relationship, then you're missing out on a wonderful part of being human.

This is where the "good stuff" portion of your personal fidelity plan comes into play. As you may recall, when we described this plan we talked about actions aimed at relationship repair *and* enjoyable activities—things you can turn to (other than cheating) that make your life fun and interesting. This is because long-term happiness, both individually and within a relationship, requires more than just sexual fidelity.

In the beginning, it may be okay for you to fill your suddenly available free time with nothing but therapy and trust-building exercises, but eventually that will get dull and boring. To avoid or escape the downward drift that so many men experience, you need to care for yourself in ways that cultivate not only your honesty and your relationship integrity, but your sense of fun and your enjoyment of life. Recognizing this, you may want to add a few (or all) of the following items to your "good stuff" list (if they aren't already on it):

- **Build solid male friendships.** Men who cheat typically have very little going on in their personal lives beyond work and their relationships with women. Many of these men have, over time, completely moved away from male friendships. However, few realize this until after they've stopped cheating for a few months. As part of the healing process, you may need to create and build friendships with other men. These connections are an opportunity to both give and receive much needed emotional support. They also give you a chance to enjoy guy stuff.
- **Spend time in nature.** Many unfaithful men say they feel alone in the healing process. Some say they've felt alone for as long as they can remember. A powerful way to realize that you aren't alone, that you are in fact part of a vast interwoven universe, is to spend time in nature. Whether it's something as simple as a daily walk in the woods or as major as a trip to the Grand Canyon, nature

shows you that we're all in this together: birds need trees for their nests, trees need soil to grow in, soil needs worms to churn it and nourish it, and so on. Nature also provides all sorts of opportunities for enjoyable time with your spouse and kids, such as camping trips, hikes, and exploring the unique resources of your area. Nature is also a wonderful place to feel connected with God.

- **Have fun.** Taking time for hobbies, games, exercise, sports, travel, quality time with family, and other enjoyable activities is an essential part of the long-term healing process. If you feel like you don't deserve to have fun after all the bad stuff you've done, it may help to think about enjoying life as part of the "daily medicine" you require to stay healthy. Regardless of whether fun is deserved, it's necessary, if for no other reason than it recharges your batteries in ways that make it easier for you to do the less enjoyable work of rebuilding trust and healing your relationship.

- **Create a "home" at home.** When cheating becomes a significant life priority, there's little time to create an environment that's warm and inviting or even to attend to routine things that need doing. In other words, cheaters tend to ignore not only their emotional (inner) selves, but their outer selves and their environment. In the process of healing, when you take some time to paint your bedroom (let your wife pick the color), plant a garden, clean the garage, build a deck, or remodel the kitchen, your outer world improves. That helps with your inner world, too, because your home becomes a source of pride as well as an enjoyable hobby.

- **Adopt and care for a pet.** Numerous studies have shown that people with pets are happier, healthier, and more connected than those without pets. This makes sense. When asked to give an example of unconditional love, many people immediately think of the love that they have

for their pet and their pet has for them. Moreover, caring for the physical and emotional needs of an animal helps to temporarily take the focus off yourself, which is usually a relief. Plus, adopting and caring for a pet is something fun that you and your spouse (and kids) can do together.
- **Hang out with your kids.** Many cheaters forget how much they love and enjoy their kids. They get so focused on cheating and keeping their infidelity secret that they withdraw from family altogether. That's a terrible shame and a gigantic missed opportunity. If you have kids around, don't miss out on the emotional miracle that active interactions can bring. Find out what interests them and nurture those interests. Feel free to share your own interests and hobbies with them. The more time you spend with your children, the stronger your bond will become. This is something you can do to rebuild your family even when your significant other is angry with and sick of you.

Of course, every guy is different, so every guy needs to create his own unique methods of self-nurturing. Gavin, for example, eventually created an amended list of goals for an enjoyable life. To the items he initially listed, he added the following:

- Join the gym and get in better physical shape.
- Work with my spouse to redecorate our home.
- Reestablish my spiritual life by going back to church and joining the men's group there.
- Find a new hobby, preferably one that I can enjoy with family and friends.
- Plan and schedule a dream vacation for next summer, and in the interim have a weekend getaway with the family. Perhaps a trip to a local attraction?
- Go out for coffee or dinner at least once every other week with my male friends and let them know what's going on in my life.

- Volunteer at least once a month for causes I believe in. Ask the kids if they want to come along and help.

As Gavin began to incorporate these goals into his life, his motivation for healing his relationship increased. His amended goals helped him understand that life after cheating can be incredibly enjoyable. He admits that he still occasionally misses the dramatic rush provided by cheating, but he's learned to appreciate the healthy pleasures of socializing with friends, providing real support to people he cares about, and developing a hobby. Rather than chasing an erratic life filled with gigantic ups and downs, he's now able to enjoy the relative peace and serenity that his reconstructed relationship provides. And the fact that he's clearly enjoying his life has made it much easier for his wife to trust that he's now being honest and faithful.

The Demanding Spouse

It's possible that your mate will somehow think that your time is now her time. She'll say, "You cheated, and now I don't trust you, so unless you're at work, you're not allowed to do anything that doesn't involve me." If so, you need to draw a line with her, perhaps with assistance from your couple's therapist. In other words, you're allowed to go golfing once in a while. No, you don't get to play 36 holes every day. But if she expects you to completely give up a hobby you enjoy, she's asking for too much. Nevertheless, you have to continue to prove that you're trustworthy in order to enjoy these pleasures. And that won't work if your former affair partner happens to also be part of your weekend golf group.

Express Gratitude to Your Spouse

As you may remember, writing a list of things you're grateful for is a great way to combat the negative emotions that tempt you toward infidelity. What we didn't tell you earlier is that sharing your gratitude list with another person—your spouse, for instance—is a wonderfully intimate act. This is doubly true if one of the items on your list is something like, "I'm grateful for the chance to rebuild relationship trust with my wife," or, "I'm grateful that I have a chance to learn and grow and become a better person." As long as you're sincere and haven't put a particular item on your gratitude list just to impress your mate, this gesture will be appreciated.

Whatever you do, don't share your gratitude list with your wife to manipulate her emotions. Betrayed partners can smell an attempt to manipulate their feelings from a mile away, and that's exactly the sort of thing that can undermine all of the other trust-building work you've been doing. That said, if and when your gratitude is sincere, you can let your mate know about it. She may not pat you on the back for it the way you'd like, but she'll certainly recognize that you're trying, and every little bit helps when you're rebuilding trust and intimacy.

Remember, the deepest gratitude comes from the heart. It's not merely as an intellectual exercise, and heart change is exactly what your spouse needs to experience from you.

When you express gratitude to your significant other, try to use *we* and *our* statements that indicate you're starting to view your life and relationship holistically, the way your mate sees it. She won't be particularly impressed when you say, "I'm grateful that I have a good job and a great house for my spouse and kids to live in," or, "I'm grateful that my kids are healthy and happy." She would much rather hear you say, "I'm grateful that we have a nice house to live in," and, "I'm grateful that our kids are healthy and seem to enjoy life."

This may seem like a subtle difference, and it is. But when it comes to rebuilding intimacy, little things mean a lot. The shift from "I" and "my" to "we" and "our" is something that your partner is certain to pick up on both consciously and subconsciously. More important, when you start reframing things in this way, your own thinking will change to reflect it. That's a shift that bodes well for the long-term health of your relationship.

View Love as a Verb

Think back to your wedding ceremony for a minute. You remember, of course, all the preparations, especially if you had a large wedding (or think about the planning still in progress if you're engaged). Smell the flowers, hear the music, and most important, picture your first glimpse of your beautiful bride. What a feeling! Most people remember their wedding day as the happiest of their life (perhaps rivaled only by the birth of a child). Without doubt, your heart was overflowing with the giddy emotions of love!

Now picture the officiant standing in front of you. If yours was like most wedding ceremonies, the clergy person read the familiar passage from 1 Corinthians 13, the "love chapter." Here it is from The Message translation by Eugene Peterson.

> *If I speak with human eloquence and angelic ecstasy but don't love, I'm nothing but the creaking of a rusty gate.*
>
> *If I speak God's Word with power, revealing all his mysteries and making everything plain as day, and if I have faith that says to a mountain, "Jump," and it jumps, but I don't love, I'm nothing.*
>
> *If I give everything I own to the poor and even go to the stake to be burned as a martyr, but I don't love, I've gotten nowhere. So, no matter what I say, what I believe, and what I do, I'm bankrupt without love.*

Love never gives up.
Love cares more for others than for self.
Love doesn't want what it doesn't have.
Love doesn't strut,
Doesn't have a swelled head,
Doesn't force itself on others,
Isn't always "Me first,"
Doesn't fly off the handle,
Doesn't keep score of the sins of others,
Doesn't revel when others grovel,
Takes pleasure in the flowering of truth,
Puts up with anything,
Trusts God always,
Always looks for the best,
Never looks back,
But keeps going to the end.

These words may not be as familiar as other translations of these verses. And if you're like most grooms, you didn't really listen to the wedding ceremony anyway, right? Take a deep breath and reread the passage slowly, maybe even out loud. It's quite a definition of love, isn't it?

We typically think of "love" as that ushy-gushy, head-over-heels *feeling*. Romantic love gets confined to the experience of limerence, which is the infatuation and obsession of early romance—the intensity of *feelings* and the desperate desire that those feelings are reciprocated. Love-as-a-feeling has its place, of course. It's an important and joyful phase of a romantic relationship. It's the kick-starter. Who'd want to enter a marriage without that rocket flame?

Love as primarily a feeling is also immature in the way we're using that word in this book. The concluding verses of 1 Corinthians 13 talk about putting away childish things, which means behaving like a mature adult. It's immature to think your sextracurricular behaviors aren't really cheating, or that they don't deeply affect your mate, or that you can mouth "I'm sorry" a few times and all will be back to normal. It's immature to expect your wife to trust you again after a few weeks (or months) of better behavior.

In the Bible love is most often used as a verb. Consider the familiar passage about God's love from John 3:16, again from The Message: "This is how much God loved the world: He gave his Son, his one and only Son. And this is why: so that no one need be destroyed; by believing in him, anyone can have a whole and lasting life." This kind of love in action is a completely different ballgame. It's self-sacrificing and gritty and very, very hard.

Love in action requires maturity and discipline. It's not based on feelings; it comes from the intention of your will. Look again at the *actions* delineated in 1 Corinthians 13. First, love "never gives up." It's easy to give up on your marriage, decide you're "in love" with your affair partner, and leave your family so you can ride off into the sunset with her. It's much, much harder to put in the work required to save your relationship.

Love "cares more for others than for self." This attribute describes the sacrifice of ego, selfishness, and immaturity that's required to rebuild a relationship your infidelity has destroyed. A covenant marriage demands a servant heart, where you put your mate's needs above your own. We're not talking about an unhealthy "codependence" where you have no sense of self or individual needs or wants. We're talking about the sacrificial attitudes and behaviors of repentance that show that you understand how much damage you've done.

Another action is pertinent here from verse four: "Love doesn't want what it doesn't have." Ouch! This concept isn't talking about your feelings. It's talking about the action of entertaining and acting on desires or temptations that take you outside your covenant relationship. This is the deepest definition of "lust," which is language used in one of the Twelve Step sexual addiction recovery fellowships. It's not just sexual lust; the concept includes going after anything that God doesn't want for you.

Consider another behavior of love that's described in 1 Corinthians 13. The Message translation says love doesn't have a "swelled head" (many Bible versions say love isn't "boastful" or "proud"). That means you don't get on your high horse and be proud that you "only" looked at porn or had virtual sex and never crossed the flesh line with another person. If you're thinking that way at this point, please start re-reading this book from the beginning.

Acting in love means you don't "force yourself on others," which in this case primarily refers to your wife. You give her the time and space she needs to heal without being impatient or demanding. You don't "fly off the handle" when she's triggered or afraid. Your attitude is no longer "Me first!" Instead, you put the wellbeing of your spouse and children first. At a deeper level, you make God first in your life, which means you live within the boundaries for sex and relationship that God established.

As crazy as it sounds considering your situation, love-as-a-verb takes pleasure in the "flowering of truth." Yes, really. That means you become grateful for the chance to live in honesty and integrity, and you embrace the path that you get to walk to become a man with those characteristics.

Love "trusts God always," which means you trust God for the outcome of this process. You can't make your spouse release you from the doghouse and decide to give your relationship another chance. Instead, you turn the outcome of this process over to a loving God and focus on taking all the steps outlined in this relationship-saving guide. You look for the best in your mate and affirm her feelings, boundaries, and healing process.

In sum, this "love chapter" is a blueprint for your changed behavior and attitude. It offers a specific guide for the kind of abiding, faithful love that lasts in the long haul.

Don't Judge Your Wife by 1 Corinthians 13

Here's an important caution: Be sure you apply these examples of love-as-a-verb to *yourself.* Resist the temptation to judge your wife's behavior by these concepts! Don't handpick the descriptions that you think she should be doing, like "love doesn't keep score of the sins of others," or, "doesn't revel when others grovel," or especially, "puts up with anything." Trust us on this one: If your spouse gets the first whiff that you're measuring her reactions with this chapter's yardstick—or worse, that you're pointing out that she isn't practicing love in action—your progress in rebuilding trust plummets. Your arrogance at bringing up your mate's flaws is as damaging as continuing to lie. *Just don't.*

Questions for Reflection

1. Do you think that you now have empathy for your wife and what you've put her through? If not, what's keeping you from developing empathy for her? (Look at your own heart, not at anything about her.) If you're not sure, ask your counselor, spiritual advisor, or a trusted friend.

2. Do you think that you and your mate can implement the respectful conflict agreement suggested in this chapter? If so, what part of the agreement do you anticipate will be most difficult for you?

3. In what ways can you engage in healthy self-care? Do you think that these areas of your life were neglected when you were cheating?

4. Which parts of 1 Corinthians 13 do you most need to implement in your life?

CHAPTER TEN

BEYOND THE DOGHOUSE

"The end of a matter is better than its beginning."
—Ecclesiastes 6:8

Better Than Before is Right Around the Corner

You may not believe this, given the current state of your relationship, but in time, if you sincerely follow the steps in this book, your relationship with your spouse can and will be better than ever. No, it won't look or feel the way it did before you cheated or while you were cheating, but that's a good thing, not a bad thing. When you become an open book with your mate and behave in trustworthy, rigorously honest ways in all facets of your life, you become much more intimate and emotionally connected. That may not seem like your primary goal right now—you probably just want to avoid divorce—but in a year or two you'll be amazed at how much you value this benefit of sticking with your mate and healing the relationship.

The redemptive process of emerging from the doghouse and entering into a different kind of relationship with your wife seems to be a new beginning, and in many ways, it is. But as Richard Rohr (2017) reminds us, the deepest transformation usually doesn't happen when something new starts, but when something old falls apart. It's the paradox of resurrection, of coming back to life after death.

To rocket yourself and your relationship into the stratosphere, two primary tasks remain: developing and strengthening non-sexual intimacy, and slowly reintroducing sex into the relationship. This is the fun part of the healing process. You will enjoy this, and your significant other will, too. This stage is the payoff for all your hard work.

Developing Non-Sexual Intimacy with Your Spouse

It's sad that our sex-obsessed culture has degraded the word intimacy by turning it into a heavily sexualized term. If you don't believe us, think about this question: *Were you intimate with your spouse last night?* In all likelihood, your immediate interpretation of that query is that we're asking if the two of you had sex. Let's do a bit of damage control with the word intimacy by defining it more accurately.

> **Intimacy is a state of honesty, vulnerability, and trust between two people.**

From this definition, you can see that intimacy isn't all about sex. In fact, it's possible to have a wonderfully intimate relationship with absolutely no sex at all. Plenty of people do, and you need intimate relationships with other men as well as with your wife. Nevertheless, in most romantic relationships sex is an expression of shared honesty, vulnerability, and trust. This is especially true for your spouse, who will literally and figuratively "open herself" to you.

Can you imagine how difficult that must be for her after you've cheated on her, betrayed her vulnerability, and ruined relationship trust? To be honest, for a good long while after you've cheated, your mate probably won't want to have sex with you. And if she does offer sex, it's likely out of fear that you might return to seeking sex outside the relationship if you're not being sexual with her. Basically, she might think that you'll eventually leave her if she doesn't provide the satisfaction you were getting elsewhere. But believe us, she won't feel good about this sex. If you take her up on such an offer, realize that you do this selfishly, and that your self-centeredness in the moment could feel like a further betrayal. That said, if your mate offers sex and you say no without explaining why, she could easily lapse into a shame spiral. In this scenario you lose either way, right?

Not exactly. The best way to approach this delicate balance is to explain that you know you've ruined relationship trust with her, at least for now, and that you've betrayed her vulnerability. Then tell her that you do find her attractive and you do want to have sex with her, but you want her to be fully comfortable with that idea before it happens. Acknowledge that you suspect you're going to have to do a lot more to rebuild trust before she gets to that place. As an alternative to having sex, suggest being intimate in a non-sexual way, such as the following:

- Holding hands and talking
- Planning a family activity together
- Taking her on a non-sexual date (e.g., dinner, a movie, a trip to the park)
- Going for a walk with her and sharing at least one important thing about your life right now
- Inviting her to look you in the eyes and tell you what she's feeling, then reciprocating after she has finished talking
- Asking her to tell you about a work project or something she is working on at home
- Doing chores together (e.g., grocery shopping, yardwork, housecleaning)
- Starting a social media page together
- Volunteering together at a local charity

- Doing something that you know she really enjoys, like antiquing or going to a museum

It doesn't matter much what you do here. The goal is to spend quality time with your spouse without turning the action to sex. Whatever you're doing, you are silently telling her that you love her, care about her, and want to be with her.

> Note: Don't wait until your significant other tries to be sexual before initiating non-sexual intimacy. Be proactive with this step to let her know that you value your entire relationship, not just the sex. And make sure you don't try to use these non-sexual forms of intimacy as foreplay. If you do that, she'll feel manipulated. When the time is right for sex, you will both know. But that may be several months down the road.

In general, the more time that partners who are trying to overcome the pain of infidelity spend together, the better. But this time shouldn't be entirely focused on hurt and healing. You need to enjoy the "good stuff" in your personal fidelity plan, and your relationship needs to experience this, too. This means having fun together—building non-sexual intimacy—in addition to the drudgework of recovery.

About Forgiveness

It's important that you understand that forgiveness is a process, not an event. It doesn't happen all at once and it's usually given only when earned, rather than when it's requested. If you want forgiveness you can apologize a million times hoping it will appear, but you won't get it until you've earned it. Much of what you're asked to consider and do in this book can help you earn it. But forgiveness isn't something you should ever expect or demand from anyone, let alone your betrayed spouse. Forgiveness will come when she can see past her broken heart, and when trust is restored.

For you, forgiveness may mean, "Phew. She loves me again and we're moving on." To her, though, it means letting you back into her heart in a way that once again puts you in a position to either love or hurt her. That's a pretty big difference! So please, give her the space she needs and let her forgive you in her own time.

In the interim, you'll have to earn her trust and forgiveness by being a good husband. This means, at minimum, that you are no longer cheating, lying, or keeping secrets, and that you are committed to a life of sexual integrity. It also means you're willing to accept her anger without being defensive, even if what she's saying feels inaccurate, undeserved, or unfair.

Forgiveness is most likely to come when you finally understand that your mate's anger, scrutiny, and distrust stem from the larger issue—your betrayal—rather than anything presenting itself in the moment. As such, your empathy and patience with her hurt and pain, along with your willingness to be honest and to not push for romance and sex before she's ready, are the things that will eventually evoke forgiveness. You'll have to feel the pain you've caused, experience your consequences without becoming defensive, and become rigorously honest in all aspects of life. If you can do that, she'll eventually forgive you—or at least you'll have done everything you can to influence that outcome. And when she does, you'll be ready to take that in and fully accept it.

Slowly Reintegrating Sex

If you're like most guys, as you work toward rebuilding relationship trust you might at least occasionally wonder if you're ever going to have hot sex again—or any sex at all, for that matter. Well, you will. In fact, if you rebuild trust and create non-sexual intimacy with your spouse, you'll eventually be very happy sexually, because intimate sex is, without doubt, the best sex you'll ever have.

When you think that it might be time to reintroduce sex into your relationship, you and you mate should do so mutually. Rebuilding sexual trust is a process, just as rebuilding relationship trust is a process. There are several things you can do to get the ball rolling, but you shouldn't try these too early—that is, before your spouse begins to trust you again. If you do, rather than appreciating your gesture, she'll wonder if you're trying to manipulate her emotions yet again. And you should never do any of these things if your actions aren't sincerely motivated by love, respect, and affection for your mate.

Things you can do that will help you reintegrate sex into your relationship include the following:

- Wake up early and do your household chores, then do hers. Don't ask for a compliment. Don't expect a compliment. Don't even bring it up. If she mentions that you've been a good boy, tell her you just wanted to get all that work stuff out of the way so the two of you could do something fun together. Then ask if there is anything she wants to do. Just in case she can't think of anything, make sure you have a few options ready (and be sure they're activities she enjoys).
- Write her a love note, telling her how much she means to you and how important your relationship is.
- Give her genuine compliments. Keep in mind that telling her she looks pretty is nice, but telling her something about her that you value—the firm but gentle hand she has with the kids, that she volunteers and tries to make the world a better place, that she's incredibly honest without ever being cruel—will mean a lot more.
- Buy her a gift. (You're now at the point where gifts given "just because" won't be questioned.) The gift shouldn't be anything big; it just has to show that you were thinking about her and the things she likes. If she's constantly

amused by your children's silly windup toys, buy her a toy of her own. If she thinks pigs are cute animals, buy her a ceramic pig. Things like chocolates, flowers, and jewelry will certainly be appreciated, of course, but not as much as something that took some thought about who she is and that you would give only to her (i.e., the sort of thing you would never have given to another woman).

- Tell her that you love her, and that you are grateful she didn't leave you when you betrayed her trust. Be clear that you know the relationship was in her hands at that point and that if she had wanted to leave you nobody would have blamed her. Thank her for choosing to give you another chance, and say that your life is richer and much more fulfilling because she did.

The point of these actions is to demonstrate to your spouse that you're paying attention to her—the real her, not the idealized or sexualized version of her—and you care about her happiness and wellbeing. A small gift or gesture that demonstrates that you "get her" is much more intimate than something extravagant. Extravagant efforts are likely to be appreciated, but she'll ultimately be happier with something smaller that is directed at her inner self.

Eventually, of course, the time will come when both you and your wife are ready for sex. The first and probably most important step is to talk about the prospect of resuming your sexual relationship. Don't just initiate sex like you did in the "before" days. Assuming that your spouse is interested in sexual activity will feel disrespectful and objectifying for her. Take the risk to invite her into a conversation about your relationship and what she wants in terms of rebuilding your sexual intimacy.

This is a delicate moment, since the emotional wounds you inflicted are probably still raw and easily reopened. It's wise to start slowly, perhaps with romantic activities that don't involve actual sex. Here are a few suggestions:

- Give each other massages, especially foot and hand massages.
- Cuddle.
- Kiss.
- Hold hands.
- Spoon before you fall asleep.
- Dress each other in the morning or before you go out together in the evening.
- Take a leisurely bath or shower together.

Soon enough, if you don't do anything that causes your spouse to believe she can't fully trust you, sex will naturally occur.

At this point, you might remember a statement we made in the opening paragraph of this section: *Intimate sex is without doubt the best sex you will ever have.* Will it be as exciting and intense as some of the sex you had when cheating? Perhaps not, but it will still be better. If we tried to fully explain why, we would have to write another book, so for now we'll just give you the shortest possible explanation: The trust and non-sexual intimacy you've built with your spouse throughout your process of healing is unbelievably powerful. It will transform sex with your wife into something you've never before experienced. Even if the sex itself is mediocre, the experience of sharing and becoming vulnerable with your mate will not be. And you'll probably find that this connection with your spouse is far more important than any orgasm, no matter how mind blowing.

We are not lying. Sex will become real in a way that seems unreal. Do you want that? If so, consider the following tips toward sexually loving your wife better:

- Stay emotionally present. If something happens that distracts one or both of you, it's okay to pause and put the sex on hold. Later, when you are both able to focus fully

on each other, you can try it again. You don't have to finish sex just for the sake of finishing sex.
- Talk to each other during sex. Let her know more about what you like and don't like. Ask her to tell you what she likes and doesn't like.
- Try having sex with the lights on and looking into each other's eyes. There are plenty of positions in which this can be done, so feel free to try something other than the standard missionary position.
- Instead of initiating sex, initiate a conversation about sex. In fact, you might even want to interview her about sex. Ask her what she enjoys about it. Ask if there are times she doesn't enjoy it, and, if so, why. Ask her what she experiences emotionally during sex. If your spouse turns the tables and asks you similar questions, answer them as openly and honestly as you can.

Creating a Better Future

If you've read this entire book, you're probably very serious about rebuilding trust and saving your relationship. If so, our hope is that you'll implement the suggestions outlined here, no matter how onerous they might initially sound or feel. If you do so, your history of infidelity can truly become the past—coloring but not leaking into your present and future. Over time, your mate will no longer experience ongoing anxiety because she's wondering when your next betrayal might occur, and you'll no longer experience ongoing anxiety because you're wondering if she'll ever trust you again. You'll be able to relax into your new intimacy, knowing that any reminders of past infidelity can also be markers of your new, much better relationship.

Of course, the process of healing from infidelity—rebuilding trust and establishing genuine intimacy—isn't easy. As we've written several times, it tends to be two steps forward, one step backward.

There will be plenty of days when you want to give up and walk away. You might even wonder whether your spouse will ever let you out of the doghouse. In those moments, when you're unable to envision a future without her pain and anger ruling the day, it's easy to lose hope. But trust us when we tell you that if you're sincere and diligent in your efforts, she will eventually come around. And when she does, your relationship, your future—and your sex life—can and almost certainly will be better than ever.

Robert Browning wrote in the poem *Rabbi Ben Ezra*, "Grow old along with me! The best is yet to be." Your relationship and your life won't go back to what you had before, but why would you want that? Your previous version of normal was broken: filled with betrayals, lack of true intimacy, secrets, and unrequited vulnerability. Wouldn't you prefer a *new normal*, in which you are fully honest with your spouse about absolutely everything, and you feel closer and more connected to her than ever?

When working with clients, we sometimes use the analogy of a broken teacup. If you drop it and it shatters, you can glue it back together, but the cracks will always show. However, those cracks don't mean that the teacup isn't still beautiful and worthwhile. Marnie has a coffee mug that was made over 35 years ago by the artist wife of a couple with whom Marnie and her husband were best friends during the early years of marriage. Both couples' children were born around the same time, and they shared many happy hours together. Eventually, the mug's handle broke when the mug was dropped one too many times, but Marnie still reaches for that glued-together mug more than any other.

Similarly, a friend of Rob's has a large painting in the entryway to his house. Once upon a time this artwork adorned the lobby of an upscale Hawaiian hotel—until a tropical storm swept through and damaged it rather badly. The outer edges were torn, and quite a bit of moisture soaked through the canvas, turning the artwork into a crackled mosaic. Rob's astute, art-collecting friend bought the damaged piece, dried it out, trimmed the badly ripped edges, re-stretched the remainder, and placed it back in its original albeit trimmed-down frame. When the hotel manager saw the new version of the painting, he begged to buy it back, because it was more beautiful than ever.

Much like a repaired teacup, mug, or painting, your repaired relationship can be more beautiful, more treasured, more loved, and more real than ever—in part *because* it was nearly ruined and discarded. That's quite an awesome paradox. It's redemption!

Scripture talks about the "mystery" of marriage, which is a word that describes the astonishing renewal that can happen when a couple recovers from infidelity. When a cheating husband puts off his "old self and its deceitful desires" and is "made new in true righteousness and holiness" (Eph. 4:22-24, paraphrased), the possibility opens for a new life. If you follow the steps and principles in this redemptive guide, you'll be way beyond simply being released from the doghouse. You'll be living as a man of integrity, with hope and a future ordained by God (Jer. 29:11).

Questions for Reflection

1. In what ways can you develop non-sexual intimacy with your mate? List at least five specific things you're willing to do.

2. What are your fears and hopes about moving forward sexually in your relationship? Are you willing to talk about these with your wife?

3. In what ways could you and your spouse be physically intimate without actually having sex (e.g., cuddling, spooning, bathing together, giving each other massages, engaging in playful sexual conversations)?

4. How could you make actual sex more intimate and therefore more rewarding? What might keep you from connecting more with your mate during sex?

5. Consider Jeremiah 29:11. "For I know the plans I have for you, declares the Lord, plans to prosper you and not to harm you, plans to give you hope and a future. Then you will call upon me and come and pray to me, and I will listen to you. You will seek me and find me when you seek me with all your heart." Write a few sentences about your hope for a redeemed future.

ADDENDUM
ABOUT DISCLOSURE

Rigorous honesty isn't just about the present and the future, it's about the past as well—including the full extent of your infidelity. However, disclosing your full history of cheating shouldn't take place without professional assistance, preferably from an experienced couple's counselor. This is true regardless of how many times your spouse says she wants to know everything right this instant.

No matter what, please do not attempt full disclosure on your own! Doing that is a horrible idea that will probably backfire. Consider the following cautionary tale.

Rich had been cheating on his wife for more than ten years with multiple women. When she finally caught him in an affair with a neighbor, she insisted that if he didn't come clean about every last detail she would immediately leave him. Rich, thinking he might feel unburdened if he just got everything out in the open, complied, answering at first in general terms. "I've been cheating off and on for ten years with several different women." Of course, with every general statement he made, his wife pushed for details. And with every detail she got, she pushed for still more information. At the end of this process, Rich's intensely depressed and angry wife packed her bags and left. The next day she filed for divorce, armed with a laundry list of his indiscretions.

Rich jumped the gun on disclosure, and the process blew up in his face. Because his well-intentioned effort to come clean wasn't properly structured and supervised—and didn't provide his wife with the support she needed and deserved—it led to a very messy and extremely expensive divorce.

Nevertheless, at some point in the healing process your spouse will likely want to know *everything* about your cheating, which is reasonable and actually healthy. A formalized, therapist-supervised process of disclosure is your best format to meet this very important need, desire, and mandate in a healthy and productive way.

> Note: If you're tempted to throw this book across the room because the last thing that you want to do is to tell your partner anything she doesn't already know, we suspect you've jumped ahead to this section. If so, we suggest you return to chapters six and seven and then finish the book. If your male friends, your dad, your brothers, and even some of the women in your life are saying that no good can come from full disclosure, they're wrong. The core message of this book is the importance of honesty, integrity, and heart change. Full disclosure of your past infidelities as well as your current cheating is a critical part of that redemptive process.

There are three important benefits of disclosure, *but only in a professional setting and only for couples who intend to stay together*:

1. You eliminate secrets and unknowns, which advances the restoration of trust.
2. You alleviate your spouse's fear that you're still lying and keeping important secrets.
3. You give your mate a chance to clearly evaluate the situation, so that after knowing the entire history of your

infidelity, she can decide in a fully informed way that she really does (or doesn't) want to stay with you.

Legitimate Reasons to Not Give Full Disclosure

There are several very good reasons not to disclose the full extent of your cheating:

- You or your spouse aren't truly interested in saving your relationship.
- Your spouse says she'd rather not know more.
- Your spouse isn't willing to let a professional guide you through the disclosure process.
- Your spouse isn't emotionally or physically healthy enough to experience this process. (Be careful not to use this reason as an excuse to avoid disclosure. You almost certainly aren't in a position to evaluate your spouse's health. Ideally both of you will meet with a qualified couples' counselor, and that professional will intervene if she or he believes that disclosure would be harmful for your wife. If so, the counselor should be able to offer your wife resources that can ultimately prepare her for disclosure, if she chooses.)
- Your spouse wants the information to use against you in a divorce or child custody dispute.

Since you've now read almost this entire book, we'll assume the first reason doesn't apply. As for the next two, if your spouse tells you that she'd rather not know any more than she already does or that she'd rather not seek help from a professional counselor, that's her choice to make. Most likely, however, she will insist on some degree of disclosure, and she will be willing to accept professional help with this process. If appropriate, invite your wife to read the following message just for her.

Wives: Of Course You Want to Know!

Please be assured that we affirm your deep pain at your husband's betrayal. We also understand your almost desperate drive to know *everything*. You're trying to make sense of your now-altered universe. You're hoping that knowledge will lessen your pain, that knowing the details will stop your questions about why and answer what you should do now.

Unfortunately, it won't. In fact, a botched disclosure will almost certainly increase your pain. Simply put, your husband just isn't capable of providing full disclosure in a healthy and productive way without help, especially if he's early in the healing process. Without professional guidance and support, he is likely to continue to tell half-truths, or worse, to outright lie or blame you somehow. Your husband is afraid of the consequences of his infidelity, and he's trying to control the damage.

We believe that you deserve to have your questions answered and to know the details that you need to know. (For example, if your husband has acted out in the hotel where you're planning to have your daughter's wedding reception, you need to know that specific information so you can decide if you're okay with that location.) Many details, though, aren't helpful, and in the middle of your terrible pain, you deserve protection from more harm.

We beg you to resist the urge to pressure your husband for immediate details about his acting out. Please believe us that an impromptu, unguided disclosure won't provide what you really want, which is an honest, complete, straightforward, and remorseful account. Please be assured that we do instruct him that he must tell you immediately if he has exposed you to a health risk or exposed your children to inappropriate activity. He must also inform you if his cheating has occurred with someone you know. (See chapter seven for more information.)

Please gift yourself with a trained counselor to help you navigate the churning waters of disclosure. You shouldn't have to wait long to receive the information you need. We recommend that your husband engage a professional and be prepared to provide disclosure within a month after his cheating becomes known. In the meantime, ask God to quiet your heart and provide the grace for you to endure this painful process. Lean on safe women for support—but be cautious about taking unschooled advice that goes against what clinical training and years of experience have taught us about disclosure.

FURTHER READING

Affair Recovery

- Carder, Dave. 2017. *Anatomy of an Affair: How Affairs, Attractions, and Addictions Develop, and How to Guard Your Marriage Against Them.* Chicago: Moody Publishers.

- Carder, Dave. 2008. *Torn Asunder: Recovering from an Extramarital Affair.* Chicago: Moody Publishers.

- Shriver, Gary, and Shriver, Mona. 2009. *Unfaithful: Hope and Healing After Infidelity.* Denair, CA: David C. Cook.

General Marriage

- Chapman, Gary. 2015. *5 Love Languages: The Secret to Love that Lasts* (5th ed.). Chicago: Northfield Publishing.

- Harley, Jr., Willard F. 2011. *His Needs, Her Needs: Building an Affair Proof Marriage* (2nd ed.). United Kingdom: Lion's Hudson Place.

- Hunt, June. 2014. *Marriage: To Have and to Hold.* Carson, CA: Rose Publishing.

- Keller, Timothy. 2013. *The Meaning of Marriage: Facing the Complexities of Commitment with the Wisdom of God.* New York: Penguin.

- Parrott, Les and Parrott, Leslie. 2015. *Saving Your Marriage Before It Starts.* Grand Rapids, MI: Zondervan.

- Smalley, Greg and Paul, Robert. 2006. *The DNA of Relationships for Couples.* Carol Stream, IL: Tyndale House.

- Thomas, Gary L. 2015. *Sacred Marriage: What if God Designed Marriage to Make Us Holy More Than to Make Us Happy?* (2nd ed.). Grand Rapids, MI: Zondervan.

- Trent, John. 2015. *30 Ways a Husband Can Bless His Wife*, Torrance, CA: Aspire Press.

- Trent, John. 2017. *30 Ways a Wife Can Bless Her Husband*, Torrance, CA, Aspire Press.

Sex

- McCluskey, Christopher. 2006. *When Two Become One: Enhancing Sexual Intimacy in Marriage.* Ada, MI: Revell.

- Penner, Cliff and Penner, Joyce. 2017. *The Married Guy's Guide to Great Sex.* Colorado Springs, CO: Focus on the Family.

- Wheat, Ed and Wheat, Gaye. 2010. *Intended for Pleasure: Sex Technique and Sexual Fulfillment in Christian Marriage* (4th ed.). Ada, MI: Revell.

Sexual/Pornography Addiction

- Ferree, Marnie C. 2010. *No Stones: Women Redeemed from Sexual Addiction* (2nd ed.). Downers Grove, IL: Intervarsity Press.

- Laaser, Debra. 2008. *Shattered Vows: Hope and Healing for Women Who Have Been Sexually Betrayed.* Grand Rapids, MI: Zondervan.

- Laaser, Mark. 2004. *Healing the Wounds of Sexual Addiction.* Grand Rapids, MI: Zondervan.

- Struthers, William. 2010. *Wired for Intimacy: How Pornography Hijacks the Male Brain.* Downers Grove, IL: Intervarsity Press.

- Weiss, R. 2015. *Sex Addiction 101: A Basic Guide to Healing from Sex, Porn, and Love Addiction.* Deerfield Beach, FL: Health Communications.

REFERENCES

Brown, B. 2012. *Daring Greatly: How the Courage to Be Vulnerable Transforms the Way We Live, Love, Parent, and Lead.* London: Penguin.

Brown, E. M. 2013. *Patterns of Infidelity and Their Treatment.* New York: Routledge.

Cacioppo, S., F. Bianchi-Demicheli, C. Frum, J. Pfaus, and J. Lewis. 2012. "The Common Neural Bases Between Sexual Desire and Love: A Multilevel Kernel Density fMRI Analysis." *Journal of Sexual Medicine* 9 (4): 1048–54.

Chivers, M. L., G. Rieger, E. Latty, and J. M. Bailey. 2004. "A Sex Difference in the Specificity of Sexual Arousal." *Psychological Science* 15 (11): 736–44.

Connell, C. M., and D. J. Lago. 1984. "Favorable Attitudes Toward Pets and Happiness Among the Elderly." In *Pet Connection: Its Influence on Our Health and Quality of Life*, edited by R. K. Anderson, B. L. Hart, and L.Hart, Minneapolis, MN: Center to Study Human Animal-Relationships and Environments.

Fisher, H. 2004. *Why We Love: The Nature and Chemistry of Romantic Love.* New York: Macmillan.

Garcia, J. R., J. MacKillop, E. L. Aller, A. M. Merriwether, D. S. Wilson, and J.K. Lum. 2010. "Associations Between Dopamine D4 Receptor Gene Variation with Both Infidelity and Sexual

Promiscuity." *PLoS One* 5 (11): e14162.

Glass, S. 2007. *Not Just Friends: Rebuilding Trust and Recovering Your Sanity After Infidelity.* New York: Simon and Schuster.

Heinrichs, M., and G. Domes. 2008. "Neuropeptides and Social Behaviour: Effects of Oxytocin and Vasopressin In Humans." *Progress in Brain Research* 170: 337–50.

Hetherington, E. M., and J. Kelly. 2003. *For Better or For Worse: Divorce Reconsidered.* New York: W. W. Norton.

Jackson, S. and J. Goodman, The Trust Triangle and Rebuilding Trust, concepts from SASH presentations, 2009-2012.

Kasl, C. D. 1999. *If the Buddha Dated: Handbook for Finding Love on a Spiritual Path.* New York: Penguin.

Kosfeld, M., M. Heinrichs, P. J. Zak, U. Fischbacher, and E. Fehr. 2005. "Oxytocin Increases Trust in Humans." *Nature* 435 (7042): 673–76.

Ogas, O., and S. Gaddam. 2011. *A Billion Wicked Thoughts: What the Internet Tells Us About Sexual Relationships.* New York: Penguin.

Rohr, Richard. 2017. "When Things Fall Apart," daily meditation, 12/29/2017, adapted from Richard Rohr with John Feister, *Hope Against Darkness: The Transforming Vision of Saint Francis in an Age of Anxiety.* Franciscan Media: 2002, 69.

Rupp, H. A., and K. Wallen. 2008. "Sex Differences in Response to Visual Sexual Stimuli: A Review." *Archives of Sexual Behavior* 37 (2): 206–18.

Schneider, J. P. 1988. *Back from Betrayal: Recovering from His Affairs.* Center City, MN: Hazelden.

Schneider, J. P., M. D. Corley, and R. K. Irons. 1998. "Surviving

Disclosure of Infidelity: Results of an International Survey of 164 Recovering Sex Addicts and Partners." *Sexual Addiction and Compulsivity* 5 (3): 189–217.

Schneider, J. P., and B. Schneider. 2004. *Sex, Lies, and Forgiveness: Couples Speaking Out on Healing from Sex Addiction*. 3rd ed. Tucson, AZ: Recovery Resources Press.

Schneider, J. P., R. Weiss, and C. Samenow. 2012. "Is It Really Cheating? Under- standing the Emotional Reactions and Clinical Treatment of Spouses and Partners Affected by Cybersex Infidelity." *Sexual Addiction and Compulsivity* 19 (1–2): 123–39.

Steffens, B. A., and R. L. Rennie. 2006. "The Traumatic Nature of Disclosure for Intimate Partners of Sexual Addicts." *Sexual Addiction and Compulsivity* 13 (2–3): 247–67.

Tennov, D. 1998. *Love and Limerence: The Experience of Being in Love*. Lanham, MD: Scarborough House.

Weiss, R. 2015. *Sex Addiction 101: A Basic Guide to Healing from Sex, Porn, and Love Addiction*. Deerfield Beach, FL: Health Communications.

Zietsch, B. P., L. Westberg, P. Santtila, and P. Jern. 2015. "Genetic Analysis of Human Extrapair Mating: Heritability, Between-Sex Correlation, and Receptor Genes for Vasopressin and Oxytocin." *Evolution and Human Behavior* 36 (2): 130–36

ABOUT THE AUTHORS

Robert Weiss LCSW, CSAT-S is a digital-age intimacy and relationships expert specializing in infidelity and addictions—most notably sex, porn, and love addiction. An internationally acknowledged clinician, he frequently serves as a subject expert on human sexuality for multiple media outlets including CNN, HLN, MSNBC, The Oprah Winfrey Network, The New York Times, The Los Angeles Times, and NPR, among others. He is the author of several highly regarded books, including "Out of the Doghouse: A Step-by-Step Relationship-Saving Guide for Men Caught Cheating," "Sex Addiction 101: A Basic Guide to Healing from Sex, Porn, and Love Addiction," "Sex Addiction 101: The Workbook," and "Cruise Control: Understanding Sex Addiction in Gay Men." He blogs regularly for Psychology Today, Huffington Post, and Psych Central. A skilled clinical educator, he routinely provides training to therapists, the US military, hospitals, and psychiatric centers in the US and abroad. Over the years, he has created and overseen more than a dozen high-end addiction and mental health treatment facilities. Currently, he is CEO of Seeking Integrity, LLC, which is being developed as an online and real-world resource for recovery from infidelity and sexual addiction. For more information or to reach Mr. Weiss, please visit his website, www.robertweissmsw.com, or follow him on Twitter, @RobWeissMSW.

Marnie C. Ferree LMFT, CSAT is a licensed marriage and family therapist in Nashville, Tennessee, where she is the founder and director of Bethesda Workshops, a faith-based clinical intensive workshop program for sex addicts, their partners, and couples affected by sexual addiction. A new offering through Bethesda Workshops is a program for teen females who are acting out sexually. The workshop she established in 1997 for female sex addicts was the first of its kind in the country. Her book *No Stones: Women Redeemed from Sexual Addiction* was the first to address sexual addiction in women from a Christian perspective. She is also the volume editor and contributing author of *Making Advances: A Comprehensive Guide for Treating Female Sex and Love Addicts*, which is the first clinical book on this topic. Marnie is the author of a workbook for female sex addicts, clinical articles in peer-reviewed journals, and numerous inspirational articles. She is a Certified Sex Addiction Therapist (CSAT) through the International Institute of Trauma and Addiction Professionals, and she served for over a dozen years on the editorial board of the *Sex Addiction & Compulsivity Journal*. She is a frequent speaker at professional and recovery conferences, churches, and schools, and has been featured on *Dateline* and in other media. For more information or to contact Marnie, visit www.BethesdaWorkshops.org.

Made in the USA
Columbia, SC
02 April 2018